# E3 Schol

MW00948626

# Surviving Biology Regents Exam

## Questions for Exam Practice

### *30 Days* of Practice Question Sets
**for the**
**NYS Biology Regents Exam / The Living Environment**
with
## Answers and Explanations

### Regents Ready

*Effiong Eyo*

## Surviving Chemistry Book Series
**Student and teacher friendly HS chem and bio books to:**

⭐ **Excite** students to study

⭐ **Engage** students in learning

⭐ **Enhance** students understanding

For more information, previews and to order
### SurvivingChem.com
## (877) 224 – 0484    info@e3chemistry.com

# Surviving Biology Regents Exam
## Questions for Exam Practice

ISBN-13:   978-1497300989

ISBN-10:   1497300983

Printed in the United States of America

**e3 Chemistry**

*E3 Scholastic Publishing*

**SurvivingChem.com**

**(877) 224 – 0484**

**info@e3chemistry.com**

---

*Now on*
NYC DOE
Famis
E-catalog

## New York City Teachers

**Our books are now listed on Famis E-catalog through Ingram**

Vendor #:  ING032000
Contract #:  7108108

# Similarities of this Regents prep book to other prep books

- All questions are from past Regents exams.
- Current Regents exams included.
- Answers and explanations included.

## But the similarities end here.

Our question and answer explanation formats are **unlike any other Regents Prep books**. Our book formats will give you, the students, a much easier and less overwhelming studying experience, as well as greater studying benefits that are certain to build your confidence and preparedness for your exam.

# Our Question Format

| Organized | Daily Sets | Categorized Sets |
|---|---|---|

- 8 organized multiple choice question sets.
- 8 organized multiple choice question sets with graphs, tables & diagrams
- 8 organized short answer question sets.
- Small numbers of Regents questions per day.
- Enough questions for almost 6 Regents exams.

# Students: Your Benefits of our Question Format

| Quick Practices | Not Overwhelming | Do More | Track Progress |
|---|---|---|---|

- ✓ Little free time is required to practice a set of questions.
- ✓ You are more likely to start practicing for your exam.
- ✓ You are more likely to finish a set of questions.
- ✓ You can do a set quickly, and correct it right away.
- ✓ You will not be or feel overwhelmed.
- ✓ You will practice a lot more Regents question
- ✓ You will encounter a lot more different types of Regents questions.
- ✓ You can easily compare your performance on the multiple choice category to that of the constructed response category.
- ✓ You can easily see and track your progress, improvement and readiness for your exam.

# Our Answer Explanation Format

| Clear | Brief | Simplified | Organized |
|-------|-------|------------|-----------|

- Brief and short (not wordy and lengthy).

- Keyword or phrase in each question clearly noted.

- Key term and/or definition necessary to answer a question clearly noted.

- Doesn't just explain, but show how to think through the question to answer it correctly.


## Students: Your Benefits of our Explanation Format

| Study Quicker | Learn Easily | Understand Better |
|---------------|--------------|-------------------|

✓ Quick and easy grading of multiple choice and constructed response

✓ You will quickly find out why you got a question wrong.

✓ You will quickly learn the concept tested by the question.

✓ You will quickly learn the keyword or phrase in the question.

✓ You will quickly learn important information needed to answer correctly.

✓ You will quickly learn how you could have thought of the question to answer it correctly.

✓ You can easily study and understand the explanation.

✓ You will have a better chance of answering similar questions correctly on your exam.

# Preparing for your Biology Regents Exam

## Months, weeks, and days before the Exam

### PAY ATTENTION AND LISTEN TO YOUR TEACHER.
Your teacher knows you better than authors of exam prep books.
Pay attention in class, and do what she or he says and recommends.

### ATTEND REVIEW SESSIONS.
Bring specific questions on concepts that you need the most help with.
You'll get more out of a review session if your questions to specific problems are answered.

### PRACTICE EXAM QUALITY QUESTIONS:  USE THIS BOOK.
Start early (a month or so) and practice a set of questions a day at a time.
Correct your answers and read up on explanations.
Keep note of points from each set to track your progress and improvement.

### STUDY YOUR NOTES AND REVIEW PACKAGES.
Focus on concepts you have problems with because you may not have enough time to study everything.
Make notes of concepts that are not clear, and bring them to your teacher.

Alternate between reviewing notes and practicing questions. It is highly recommended that you spend more of your time practicing questions.

### BE FAMILIAR WITH THE CURRENT EXAM AND SCORING FORMATS.
Be sure to do and grade the two recent Regents Exams on Days 27 to 30.
Doing and correcting them will give you a great sense of what to expect on the test, and how your test will be graded.

## Night before the exam
Get a good night sleep, Relax!

## Day of the exam
Eat a good meal. Relax!
Bring sharpened pencils, pens, and a calculator.

## During the exam
Relax! Read and think through each question and choice thoroughly.
You know the answer to that question because you've worked hard and been taught well.

### You've Got Bio ☺

### Good Luck!

# Table of Contents

Start small.

Build confidence.

Finish strong.

Start: Answer all questions on this day before stopping.

1. Two closely related species of birds live in the same tree. Species *A* feeds on ants and termites, while species *B* feeds on caterpillars. The two species coexist successfully because

(1) each occupies a different niche
(2) they interbreed
(3) they use different methods of reproduction
(4) birds compete for food

2. A human liver cell is very different in structure and function from a nerve cell in the same person. This is best explained by the fact that

(1) different genes function in each type of cell
(2) liver cells can reproduce while the nerve cells cannot
(3) liver cells contain fewer chromosomes than nerve cells
(4) different DNA is present in each type of cell

3. The levels of organization for structure and function in the human body from least complex to most complex are

(1) systems $\rightarrow$ organs $\rightarrow$ tissues $\rightarrow$ cells
(2) cells $\rightarrow$ organs $\rightarrow$ tissues $\rightarrow$ systems
(3) tissues $\rightarrow$ systems $\rightarrow$ cells $\rightarrow$ organs
(4) cells $\rightarrow$ tissues $\rightarrow$ organs $\rightarrow$ systems

4. After a rabbit population reaches the carrying capacity of its habitat, the population of rabbits will most likely

(1) decrease, only
(2) increase, only
(3) alternately increase and decrease
(4) remain unchanged

5. Much of the carbon dioxide produced by green plants is *not* excreted as a metabolic waste because it

(1) can be used for photosynthesis
(2) is too large to pass through cell membranes
(3) is needed for cellular respiration
(4) can be used for the synthesis of proteins

6. Which part of a molecule provides energy for life processes?

(1) carbon atoms                    (3) chemical bonds
(2) oxygen atoms                    (4) inorganic nitrogen

7. To increase chances for a successful organ transplant, the person receiving the organ should be given special medications. The purpose of these medications is to

(1) increase the immune response in the person receiving the transplant
(2) decrease the immune response in the person receiving the transplant
(3) decrease mutations in the person receiving the transplant
(4) increase mutations in the person receiving the transplant

8. Competition between two species occurs when

(1) mold grows on a tree that has fallen in the forest
(2) chipmunks and squirrels eat sunflower seeds in a garden
(3) a crow feeds on the remains of a rabbit killed on the road
(4) a lion stalks, kills, and eats an antelope

9. In order to reduce consumption of nonrenewable resources, humans could

(1) burn coal to heat houses instead of using oil
(2) heat household water with solar radiation
(3) increase industrialization
(4) use a natural-gas grill to barbecue instead of using charcoal

10. Four environmental factors are listed below.
          *A.* energy
          *B.* water
          *C.* oxygen
          *D.* minerals
Which factors limit environmental carrying capacity in a land ecosystem?

(1) *A,* only                    (3) *A, C,* and *D,* only
(2) *B, C,* and *D,* only        (4) *A, B, C,* and *D*

**Day 1**

**Stop.** Check your answers and note how many correct **Points**

| **Day 1** | **Multiple Choice Questions** |
|:---|---:|
| **10 Points** | ***Answers and Explanations*** |

1. **1**      Each of the two species feeds on different insects on the same habitat (tree), therefore, they two species are not in competition.

     Not in competition = different niche (functions ) in a habitat.

2. **1**      The word *gene* in Choice 1 best describes why the two cells have different functions and structures.

     A gene is a unit of heredity that holds instructions (genetic codes) for building and maintaining cells to perform certain function.

     One cell is different from another because each cell type contains a unique set of genes (or instructions).

3. **4**      C-TOS      **C**ell – least complex
     **T**issue
     **O**rgan
     **S**ystem – most complex

4. **3**      Population homeostasis (stability) of any organism is maintained by alternating increase and decrease in the number of organism in the ecosystem.

     Periodic increase is due to birth.
     Periodic decrease is due to death .

     *Population homeostasis* is necessary for the survival of the rabbit (or any) species.

5. **1**      *Carbon dioxide, $CO_2$, is needed for photosynthesis.*

     $CO_2 + H_2O + energy \rightarrow C_6H_{12}O_6 + O_2$    (photosynthesis)

     $CO_2$ produced by plants in other life processes can be recycled and reused in photosynthesis .

6. **3**  Chemical bonds hold atoms of molecules together.

Potential energy is stored in *chemical bonds* of molecules.

Energy is released for life processes when these bonds are broken.

7. **2**  Transplant = putting foreign organ into the organ-recipient.

Foreign organ triggers immune response in organ-recipients.

*Specialized medications decrease immune response* (or lessen chance of rejection) and increase a chance of successful transplant.

Choice 1 is incorrect because an increase immune response means increase chance of rejection.

Choice 3 and 4 are incorrect because mutations have nothing to do with organ transplants.

8. **2**  Competition occurs when different species in the same habitat attempt to use the same resources for survival.

Only Choice 2 indicates different species (the chipmunks and squirrels) using the same resource (sunflower seeds) in the same habitat (garden).

9. **2**  One way of "reducing consumption of nonrenewable resources" is to use renewable resources for the same purpose.
Solar (sun) energy is a renewable resource than can be used as a heat source in place of burning oil, coal and natural gases (nonrenewable resources).

10. **4**  All four factors are necessary for the survival of species, and all four can be used up if population of species gets too large in the land ecosystem.

Carrying capacity in a land ecosystem, therefore, depends on all four factors.

Start:  Answer all questions on this day before stopping.

1. In the diagram below, what does *X* most likely represent?

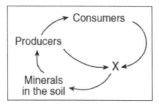

(1) autotrophs                    (3) decomposers
(2) herbivores                    (4) carnivores

2. The illustration below shows an insect resting on some green leaves. The size, shape, and green color of this insect are adaptations that would most likely help the insect to

(1) compete successfully with all birds
(2) make its own food
(3) hide from predators
(4) avoid toxic waste materials

3. Which cell structure contains information needed for protein synthesis?

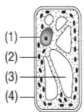

4. The diagram below represents a biochemical process. Which molecule is represented by *X*?

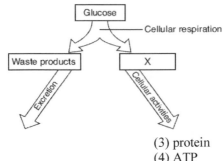

(1) DNA                                     (3) protein
(2) starch                                  (4) ATP

5. Which statement best explains the change shown in the diagram below?

(1) Gene expression in an organism can be modified by interactions with the environment.
(2) Certain rabbits produce mutations that affect genes in specific areas of the body.
(3) Sorting and recombination of genes can be influenced by very cold temperatures.
(4) Molecular arrangement in existing proteins can be altered by environmental factors.

6. Which graph represents a population that grew and is maintained at the carrying capacity of its ecosystem?

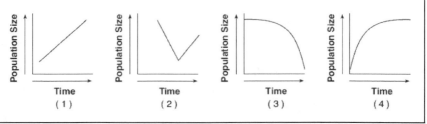

7. The diagram below represents a common laboratory technique in molecular genetics.

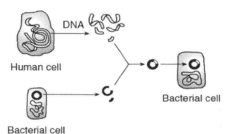

One common use of this technology is the

(1) production of a human embryo to aid women who are unable to have children
(2) change of single-celled organisms to multicellular organisms
(3) introduction of a toxic substance to kill bacterial cells
(4) production of hormones or enzymes to replace missing human body chemicals

*Base your answers to questions 8 and 9 on the diagram below, which represents stages in the digestion of a starch, and on your knowledge of biology.*

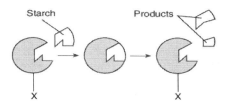

8. The products would most likely contain

(1) simple sugars          (3) amino acids
(2) fats                   (4) minerals

9. The structure labeled *X* most likely represents

(1) an antibody            (3) an enzyme
(2) a receptor molecule    (4) a hormone

10. The arrows in the diagram below illustrate processes in the life of a species that reproduces sexually.

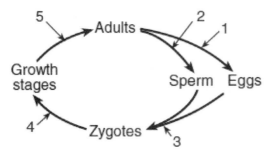

Which processes result directly in the formation of cells with half the amount of genetic material that is characteristic of the species?

(1) 1 and 2                     (3) 3 and 4
(2) 2 and 3                     (4) 4 and 5

Day 2

**Stop.** Check your answers and note how many correct **Points**

**1. 3**      In the food chain diagram shown, X derive their energy from producers (green plants) and consumers (animals).
Of all the organisms listed, *only* decomposers ( X ) derive their energy from decayed plants and animal tissues.

When decomposers died they leave behind minerals in the soil. Producers then use these minerals to grow and start the food chain cycle all over again .

**2. 3**      In the diagram shown, the insect is blended in *(camouflaged )* with the patterns on the leaves.

Camouflaged = hide

By adapting features such as shape, size, and colors that allow for blending in with its environment, the insect can *hide, and remain unnoticed from predators. (choice 3)*

These adaptation features are not necessary for any of the other three behaviors of the insect listed in choices 1,2 and 4.

**3. 2**      Protein synthesis occurs in the ribosomes of cells (2)

Structure 1 is the nucleolus (contains chromosome)
Structure 3 is the vacuole (stores nutrient materials)
Structure 4 is the cell wall (protects the cell)

**4. 4**      Cellular respiration

$$C_6H_{12}O_6 \; + \; O_2 \; \rightarrow \qquad CO_2 \; + \; H_2O \; + \; ATP$$
$$glucose \qquad oxygen \qquad\qquad waste\ products \qquad X$$
$$energy$$

**5. 1**      The obvious thing about this diagram is the color change of the rabbit's fur from white to black where the ice pack was placed.

Characteristics (such as eye color, skin color, fur color) of an individual are results of gene expressions.

Environmental factors such as temperature change (ice pack) can alter gene expression, hence , change in characteristics (white to black fur) of an individual.

6. **4**       The key information in this question is that population "grew and is maintained."

Only Choice 4 graph shows a rapid population increase (growth) and leveling off (is maintained) at a certain population size (carrying capacity).

7. **4**       The process depicted in the diagram is known as *Recombinant DNA.*

In Recombinant DNA processes, a portion of a DNA is moved from the donor cell (human) to the recipient cell (bacteria).
This process will allow the bacteria cell to rapidly produce chemicals (hormones or enzymes) that the DNA section is coded to produce.

8. **1**       In the diagram, the products are smaller units of the starch.

Starches are complex carbohydrates, which are composed of smaller and simpler molecules of sugar.

9. **3**       In the diagram, substance X is unchanged during the chemical breakdown of the starch.

Substances that are unchanged during biological processes are called enzymes (biological catalysts).

X is an enzyme because it is unchanged

10. **1**      Egg cell (produced by process 1) and sperm cell (produced by process 2) each contains half the genetic materials of an individual as a result of meiosis.

**Start:** Answer all questions on this day before stopping.

1. Acetylcholine is a chemical secreted at the ends of nerve cells. This chemical helps to send nerve signals across synapses (spaces between nerve cells). After the signal passes across a synapse, an enzyme breaks down the acetylcholine. LSD is a drug that blocks the action of this enzyme. Describe *one* possible effect of LSD on the action of acetylcholine. [1]

_____

_____

2. Mice store only a small amount of the energy they obtain from plants they eat. State what might happen to some of the remaining energy they obtain from the plants. [1]

_____

_____

3. State *one* reason that most foods must be digested before they can enter a cell. [1]

_____

_____

4. Cell A shown below is a typical red onion cell in water on a slide viewed with a compound light microscope.

Cell A

Draw a diagram of how cell A would most likely look after salt water has been added to the slide and label the cell membrane in your diagram. [2]

*Base your answers to questions 5 and 6 on the information and data table below and on your knowledge of biology.*

A student cut three identical slices from a potato. She determined the mass of each slice. She then placed them in labeled beakers and added a different solution to each beaker. After 30 minutes, she removed each potato slice from its solution, removed the excess liquid with a paper towel, and determined the mass of each slice. The change in mass was calculated and the results are shown in the data table below.

### Change in Mass of Potato in Different Solutions

| Beaker | Solution | Change in Mass |
|--------|----------|----------------|
| 1 | distilled water | gained 4.0 grams |
| 2 | 6% salt solution | lost 0.4 gram |
| 3 | 16% salt solution | lost 4.7 grams |

5. Identify the process that is responsible for the change in mass of each of the three slices. [1]

_____

6. Explain why the potato slice in beaker 1 increased in mass. [1]

_____

_____

_____

## Day 3                                                  Continue.

*Base your answers to questions 7 through 9 on the diagram below and on your knowledge of biology. The diagram shows the results of a technique used to analyze DNA.*

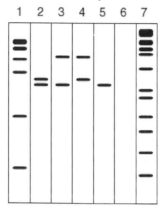

7. This technique used to analyze DNA directly results in
   (1) synthesizing large fragments of DNA
   (2) separating DNA fragments on the basis of size
   (3) producing genetically engineered DNA molecules
   (4) removing the larger DNA fragments from the samples

8. This laboratory technique is known as
   (1) gel electrophoresis
   (2) DNA replication
   (3) protein synthesis
   (4) genetic recombination

9. State *one* specific way the results of this laboratory technique could be used. [1]

_____

_____

### Day 3

**Stop.** Check your answers and note how many correct **Points**

1. **1 point**    According to the paragraph:
Acetylcholine helps to carry nerve signals.
A special enzyme is present to destroy acetylcholine.
LSD blocks action of the enzyme that destroys acetylcholine.

*Question:* What is the indirect effect of LSD on action of acetylcholine

**Acceptable responses include, *but* not limited to .**

*The work of acetylcholine would occur continuously.*

*Nerve signals would not be turned off.*

*Cell communication would not be disrupted.*


2. **1 point**    Energy is needed for many life functions of living organisms.

**Acceptable responses include, but not limited to:**

*Much of the energy is lost as heat (during cellular respiration).*
*Some of the energy is used by the mice for life functions.*


3. **1 point**    Nutrients in food are made up of large molecules.

Digestion breaks down these large molecules into smaller ones,

**Acceptable responses include, but not limited to:**

*Certain food molecules are too large to pass through the cell membrane.*

*Only small molecules can pass through cell membranes.*

**4. 2 point**    A cell placed in hypertonic solution (salt water) will lose water through osmosis. This lost of water causes the internal compartment (cytoplasm) to shrink and pull away from the cell wall.

**Since your diagram will vary from example shown below, Acceptable drawing must show:**

. *The cytoplasm of the cell should be plasmolyzed (smaller, rounded) with the cell membrane away from the cell wall.* **(1 point)**

. *The cell membrane should be clearly labeled.* **(1 point)**

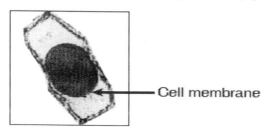

Cell membrane

**5. 1 point**    Based on the data given, the change in mass is due to movement of water either into a potato slice (Beaker 1) or out of a potato slice (Beaker 2 and 3).

**Acceptable response will be any process that describes movement of water from one area to another.**

*Osmosis*

*Diffusion*

*Passive transport*

**6. 1 point**    There is a higher concentration of water in Beaker 1 (distilled water) than inside a potato slice.

**Acceptable responses include, but are not limited to:**

*Water diffused into the cells of the potato because there is a higher concentration of water outside than inside the slice.*

*The potato slice increased in water content.*

7. **1 point**    *3*

The diagram shown is from a result of gel electrophoresis.

*Gel electrophoresis separates fragments of a biological molecule (such as DNA) by sizes. Largest size fragments on top, smallest size fragments at the bottom.*

8. **1 point**    *1*

During **gel electrophoresis process,** samples containing a mixture of polarized DNA fragments are separated (by electrical current) according to their sizes.

Electric field is then used to pull the polarized fragments through the gel. Smaller size DNA fragments move faster and appear as blots at the bottom. Larger size DNA fragments move a little slower and appear as blots closer to the top.

9. **1 point**    The purpose of gel electrophoresis is to separate DNA fragments by size, and then compare the blot patterns to that of a known source.

*Question is:* For what purpose would one compare DNA patterns?

**Acceptable responses include, but are not limited to:**

*Determining evolutionary relationships*

*Gene testing for diagnosis*

*Paternity testing*

*Determining identity*

*Solving crimes*

Start: Answer all questions on this day before stopping.

1. In order to produce the first white marigold flower, growers began with the lightest yellow flowered marigold plants. After crossing them, these plants produced seeds, which were planted, and only the offspring with very light yellow flowers were used to produce the next generation. Repeating this process over many years, growers finally produced a marigold flower that is considered the first white variety of its species. This procedure is known as

(1) differentiation          (3) gene insertion
(2) cloning                      (4) selective breeding

2. Which structures are listed in order from the least complex to the most complex?

(1) plant cell, leaf, chloroplast, rose bush
(2) chloroplast, plant cell, leaf, rose bush
(3) chloroplast, leaf, plant cell, rose bush
(4) rose bush, leaf, plant cell, chloroplast

3. Viruses frequently infect bacteria and insert new genes into the genetic material of the bacteria. When these infected bacteria reproduce asexually, which genes would most likely be passed on?

(1) only the new genes
(2) only the original genes
(3) both the original and the new genes
(4) neither the original nor the new genes

4. German measles is a disease that can harm an embryo if the mother is infected in the early stages of pregnancy because the virus that causes German measles is able to

(1) be absorbed by the embryo from the mother's milk
(2) be transported to the embryo in red blood cells
(3) pass across the placenta
(4) infect the eggs

5. The Florida panther, a member of the cat family, has a population of fewer than 100 individuals and has limited genetic variation. Which inference based on this information is valid?
(1) These animals will begin to evolve rapidly.
(2) Over time, these animals will become less likely to survive in a changing environment.
(3) These animals are easily able to adapt to the environment.
(4) Over time, these animals will become more likely to be resistant to disease

**19**

6. The relationship that exists when athlete's foot fungus grows on a human is an example of

(1) predator/prey
(2) producer/consumer
(3) parasite/host
(4) decomposer/autotroph

7. Which statement correctly describes the genetic makeup of the sperm cells produced by a human male?

(1) Each cell has pairs of chromosomes and the cells are usually genetically identical.
(2) Each cell has pairs of chromosomes and the cells are usually genetically different.
(3) Each cell has half the normal number of chromosomes and the cells are usually genetically identical.
(4) Each cell has half the normal number of chromosomes and the cells are usually genetically different.

8. A student prepared a slide of pollen grains from a flower. First the pollen was viewed through the low-power objective lens and then, without moving the slide, viewed through the high-power objective lens of a compound light microscope. Which statement best describes the relative number and appearance of the pollen grains observed using these two objectives?

(1) low power: 25 small pollen grains high power: 100 large pollen grains
(2) low power: 100 small pollen grains high power: 25 large pollen grains
(3) low power: 25 large pollen grains high power: 100 small pollen grains
(4) low power: 100 large pollen grains high power: 25 small pollen grains

9. The direct source of ATP for the development of a fetus is

(1) a series of chemical activities that take place in the mitochondria of fetal cells
(2) a series of chemical activities that take place in the mitochondria of the uterine cells
(3) the transport of nutrients by the cytoplasm of the stomach cells of the mother
(4) the transport of nutrients by the cytoplasm of the stomach cells of the fetus

10. The sweet taste of freshly picked corn is due to the high sugar content in the kernels. Enzyme action converts about 50% of the sugar to starch within one day after picking. To preserve its sweetness, the freshly picked corn is immersed in boiling water for a few minutes, and then cooled. Which statement most likely explains why the boiled corn kernels remain sweet?

(1) Boiling destroys sugar molecules so they cannot be converted to starch.
(2) Boiling kills a fungus on the corn that is needed to convert sugar to starch.
(3) Boiling activates the enzyme that converts amino acids to sugar.
(4) Boiling deactivates the enzyme responsible for converting sugar to starch.

**Day 4**

**Stop.** Check your answers and note how many correct **Points**

1. **4**      The question describes how farmers **select** a marigold of a specific characteristic from one generation to produce **(breed)** seeds for the next generation.

2. **2**      Based on the choices given, the list must start with **chloroplast** because it is a cell organelle, hence, the least complex of the structures. *Eliminate Choices 1 and 4.*

    Of the two remaining Choices, Choice 2 is best because a **plant cell** is less complex than a **leaf**, which is less complex than the whole **bush.**

3. **3**      When a foreign gene (from virus) is inserted into a genetic material of the host (bacteria), the foreign gene becomes part of the host gene.

    When the bacteria undergo asexual reproduction, all genes in the bacteria (both foreign and original) will be replicated, and then pass on to the next generation of offsprings.

4. **3**      The only connection of a developing embryo to the mother is through the placenta.

    Functions of placenta include transporting nutrients, wastes and gases between the mother and embryo. However, harmful agents like viruses can also pass through from mother to embryo.

5. **2**      The key phrase in this question is "genetic variation."

    Genetic variation = new characteri*stics*

6. **3**      In athlete's foot fungus –human relationship, the fungus (parasite) is benefited while the human (host) is harmed.

7. **4**       A sperm cell contains half the chromosomes.
The egg cell contains the other half.

Sperm cells are genetically different because they can carry either the X or Y chromosome for determining sex of offsprings.

8. **2**       Under Low Power objective lens, an object (pollen grain) will appear much smaller than when it is viewed under High Power lens.

Low Power  = Smaller grains  = More in viewing area (100)

High Power = Larger grains  = Fewer in viewing area (25)

9. **1**       ATP (energy molecule) is produced during cellular respiration, which occurs in the mitochondria.
*(Eliminate Choices 3 and 4)*

Of the two remaining choices, Choice 1 is best because energy can't be transported from mother to fetus. *The fetal cell mitochondria, therefore, must make energy for the developing fetus.*

Nutrients and chemical substances needed by the fetus to make ATP are transported from the mother to the fetus through the placenta.

10. **4**       *According to the question:*
- Sweetness of corn is due to high sugar content.

- Enzyme actions convert sugar to starch, making corn less sweet after a day.

- Corn is put in boiling water to preserve its sweetness.

*Conclusion:* Boiling water deactivates (stops) the enzyme actions on sugar.

    

Start: Answer all questions on this day before stopping.

1. The diagram below represents levels of organization in living things. Which term would best represent *X*?

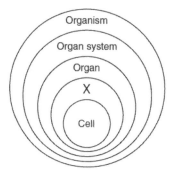

(1) human
(2) tissue

(3) stomach
(4) organelle

2. Which process is illustrated in the diagram below?

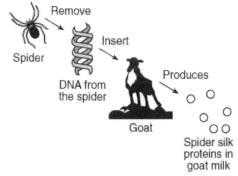

(1) chromatography
(2) direct harvesting
(3) meiosis
(4) genetic engineering

3. Some cells involved in the process of reproduction are represented in the diagram below.

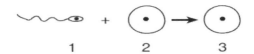

The process of meiosis formed

(1) cell 1, only                 (3) cell 3, only
(2) cells 1 and 2            (4) cells 2 and 3

4. An evolutionary pathway is represented below. Which statement about evolutionary pathways is most accurate?

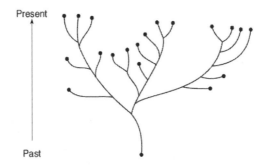

(1) All evolutionary pathways show that life began with autotrophic organisms that soon evolved into heterotrophic organisms.
(2) Two organisms on the same branch of an evolutionary pathway are more closely related to each other than to those on distant branches.
(3) All the organisms shown at the ends of evolutionary pathway branch tips are alive today.
(4) Evolutionary pathways show that evolution is a short-term process.

5. Which species in the chart below is most likely to have the fastest rate of evolution?

| Species | Reproductive Rate | Environment |
|---------|-------------------|-------------|
| A | slow | stable |
| B | slow | changing |
| C | fast | stable |
| D | fast | changing |

(1) *A*                          (3) *C*
(2) *B*                          (4) *D*

6. Two types of human cells are shown in the diagram below.

Nerve cell

Muscle cells that
attach to the skeleton

A                                                          B

Cell *A* causes the cells at *B* to contract. This activity would be most useful for

(1) lifting a book from a bookshelf
(2) coordinating the functions of organelles
(3) digesting food in the small intestine
(4) carrying out the process of protein synthesis

7. Information concerning the diet of crocodiles of different sizes is contained in the table below.

Percentage of Crocodiles of Different Lengths and Their Food Sources

| Food Source | Group A 0.3–0.5 Meter | Group B 2.5–3.9 Meters | Group C 4.5–5.0 Meters |
|---|---|---|---|
| mammals | 0 | 18 | 65 |
| reptiles | 0 | 17 | 48 |
| fish | 0 | 62 | 38 |
| birds | 0 | 17 | 0 |
| snails | 0 | 25 | 0 |
| shellfish | 0 | 5 | 0 |
| spiders | 20 | 0 | 0 |
| frogs | 35 | 0 | 0 |
| insects | 100 | 2 | 0 |

Which statement is *not* a valid conclusion based on the data?

(1) Overharvesting of fish could have a negative impact on group *C*.
(2) The smaller the crocodile is, the larger the prey.
(3) Group *B* has no preference between reptiles and birds.
(4) Spraying insecticides would have the most direct impact on group *A*.

8. The letters in the diagram below represent structures in a human female.

Estrogen and progesterone increase the chance for successful fetal development by regulating activities within structure

(1) *A*                        (3) *C*
(2) *B*                        (4) *D*

*Base your answers to questions 9 and 10 on the diagram below and on your knowledge of biology. The diagram illustrates a process by which energy is released in organisms.*

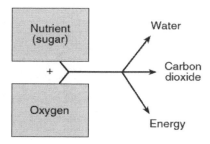

9. Cells usually transfer the energy that is released directly to

(1) glucose                   (3) oxygen
(2) ATP                        (4) enzymes

10. The energy released in this process was originally present in

(1) sunlight and then transferred to sugar
(2) sunlight and then transferred to oxygen
(3) the oxygen and then transferred to sugar
(4) the sugar and then transferred to oxygen

**Day 5**

**Stop.** Check your answers and note how many correct **Points**

1. **2**   *C-TOS*        Cell  -  least complex
                          Tissue (X)
                          Organ
                          System - most complex

2. **4**   According to the diagram, the gene for silk production
           is moved from the spider to the goat.

           The process of moving a gene from one organism to
           another is a common technique  in *genetic engineering.*

3. **2**   Meiosis is a process by which four monoploids (cells with
           half the chromosomes) are formed from a diploid nucleus.

           Sperm (1) and egg (2) are monoploid cells resulting
           from meiosis.

           3 is a zygote, a diploid cell, which is a result of fertilization
           of egg by sperm.

4. **2**   Evolutionary pathway (tree) is commonly used to show
           how organisms from a common ancestor relate to one
           another.

           Of the statements given as choices, only Choice 2 is an
           accurate conclusion that can be made of an evolutionary tree.

5. **4**   Evolution  =  gradual change of a species through time.

           Species with fast reproductive rates will go through changes
           (evolution) more rapidly than those with slow reproductive
           rates. *Eliminate Species A and B*

           Of the two remaining Species,  the Species in a *changing
           environment (D) will evolve more rapidly* (so to adapt) than
           those in a stable environment (C).

6. **1**   The key information depicted in the diagram is that muscle cells are attached to skeleton.
Skeletal movements in the arm are necessary for lifting.

Skeletal movements are NOT directly involved in functions described in Choices 2, 3 and 4.

7. **2**   Based on the information from the table, small size crocodiles (as indicated by their lengths in meters) eat small size prey. Big size crocodiles eat bigger size prey.

Choice 2 statement is, therefore, an invalid conclusion.

All other statements are correct based on the data.

8. **1**   Fetal development in human (and in all placental mammals) occurs in the uterus.

*Structure A* = *uterus(fetal development)*
Structure B = vagina (birth canal)
Structure C = fallopian tube (where fertilization occurs)
Structure D = bladder (collects and stores urine)

9. **2**   The process represented in the diagram is cellular respiration. Energy from cellular respiration is in the form of ATP.

10. **1**   Energy from cellular respiration is from oxidation of glucose (sugar, $C_6H_{12}O_6$ ). *Eliminate Choices 2 and 3.*
Sugar is produced from photosynthesis, which requires sunlight energy

sun energy absorbed     photosynthesis
$$\text{Energy} + CO_2 + H_2O \xrightleftharpoons{} C_6H_{12}O_6 + O_2$$
ATP energy released     cellular respiration

Start: Answer all questions on this day before stopping.

1. Many plants can affect the growth of other plants near them. This can occur when one plant produces a chemical that affects another plant. Design an experiment to determine if a solution containing ground-up goldenrod plants has an effect on the growth of radish seedlings. In your experimental design be sure to:
   • state a hypothesis to be tested [1]
   • describe how the experimental group will be treated differently from the control group [1]
   • explain why the number of seedlings used for the experiment should be large [1]
   • identify the type of data that will be collected [1]
   • describe experimental results that would support your hypothesis [1]

   _____

   _____

   _____

   _____

   _____

   _____

2. A chromatography setup is shown below. Identify *one* error in the setup. [1]

Stopper

Test tube

Chromatography paper

Pigment mixture spot

Solvent

*Base your answers to questions 3 through 6 on the information and data table below and on your knowledge of biology.*

A number of bean seeds planted at the same time produced plants that were later divided into two groups, *A* and *B*. Each plant in group *A* was treated with the same concentration of gibberellic acid (a plant hormone). The plants in group *B* were not treated with gibberellic acid. All other growth conditions were kept constant. The height of each plant was measured on 5 consecutive days, and the average height of each group was recorded in the data table below.

Data Table

|  | Average Plant Height (cm) | | | | |
|---|---|---|---|---|---|
|  | Day 1 | Day 2 | Day 3 | Day 4 | Day 5 |
| Group A | 5 | 7 | 10 | 13 | 15 |
| Group B | 5 | 6 | 6.5 | 7 | 7.5 |

*Directions (3 – 5): Using the information in the data table, construct a line graph on the grid on the next page, following the directions below.*

3. Mark an appropriate scale on the axis labeled "Average Plant Height (cm)." [1]

4. Plot the data for the average height of the plants in group *A*. Surround each point with a small circle and connect the points. [1]

Example:

5. Plot the data for the average height of the plants in group *B*. Surround each point with a small triangle and connect the points. [1]

Example:

**Plant Height**

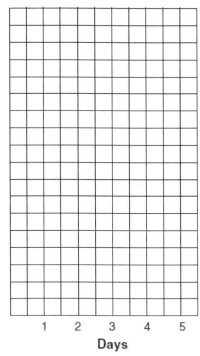

Average Plant Height (cm)

**Key**

⊙ Group A

△ Group B

Days

1    2    3    4    5

6. State a valid conclusion that can be drawn concerning the effect of gibberellic acid on bean plant growth. [1]

_____

_____

_____

**Day 6**

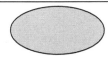

**Stop.** Check your answers and note how many correct **Points**

1. **5 points**

   **Experimental design will vary.**

   **Acceptable responses for each point category are listed below, but are not limited to what are listed:**

   **Stating the hypothesis (1 point)**

   *Radish seedlings grow faster when exposed to goldenrod solution.*

   *Radish seedlings treated with the solution will not grow as tall as the control group.*

   *The solution will not affect the height of radish seedlings.*

   NOTE: Your hypothesis should not be in a form of a question.

   **Describing Experimental and Control Group (1 point)**

   *The experimental group will be given the solution while the control group is given plain water.*

   *The experimental group will have ground up goldenrod in the soil.*

   **Explaining why large number of seedling should be used (1 point)**

   *A large sample will increase the validity of the results.*

   *Since some may die, there will be enough left to do the experiment.*

   **Identifying the type of data that will be collected (1 point)**

   *The number of seedlings that survive in each group will be counted.*

   *The height of the seedlings.*

   NOTE: Type of data must be measureable or countable

   **Describing experiment results that would support your stated hypothesis (1 point)**

   *Radish seedlings exposed to goldenrod solution were twice as tall as the control group*

   *Radish seedlings treated with the solution did not grow as tall as those in the control*

   NOTE: Your experimental result must relate to your stated hypothesis

| Day 6 | Answers and Explanations |
|---|---|

2. **1 point**    The pigment spot should be above the solvent.

                    **ERROR:** The pigment mixture spot is in the solvent.

3. **1 point**    *For marking the y-axis* evenly with numbers corresponding to "Average Plant Height" given on the Data Table.

4. **1 point**    *For plotting the data for the average height of the plants in group A,* surrounding each point with a small circle, and connecting the points.

5. **1 point**    *For plotting the data for the average height of the plants in group B,* surrounding each point with a small triangle, and connecting the points.

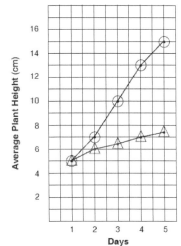

Plant Height

**Example of a 3-point graph for questions 3 through 5**

6. **1 point**    **For stating a correct conclusion** based on the data or graph.

                    **Acceptable responses include, but are not limited to:**

                    *Bean plants given gibberellic acid grew taller or faster than those that were not.*

**Start:** Answer all questions on this day before stopping.

1. After a hormone enters the bloodstream, it is transported throughout the body, but the hormone affects only certain cells. The reason only certain cells are affected is that the membranes of these cells have specific

   (1) receptors                    (3) antibodies
   (2) tissues                      (4) carbohydrates

2. Asexually reproducing organisms pass on hereditary information as

   (1) sequences of A, T, C, and G
   (2) chains of complex amino acids
   (3) folded protein molecules
   (4) simple inorganic sugars

3. In a group of mushrooms exposed to a poisonous chemical, only a few of the mushrooms survived. The best explanation for the resistance of the surviving mushrooms is that the resistance

   (1) was transmitted to the mushrooms from the poisonous chemical
   (2) resulted from the presence of mutations in the mushrooms
   (3) was transferred through the food web to the mushrooms
   (4) developed in response to the poisonous chemical

4. Experiments revealed the following information about a certain molecule:
   — It can be broken down into amino acids.
   — It can break down proteins into amino acids.
   — It is found in high concentrations in the small intestine of humans.

   This molecule is most likely

   (1) an enzyme                    (3) a hormone
   (2) an inorganic compound        (4) an antigen

5. In 1859, a small colony of 24 rabbits was brought to Australia. By 1928 it was estimated that there were 500 million rabbits in a 1-million square mile section of Australia. Which statement describes a condition that probably contributed to the increase in the rabbit population?

   (1) The rabbits were affected by many limiting factors.
   (2) The rabbits reproduced by asexual reproduction.
   (3) The rabbits were unable to adapt to the environment.
   (4) The rabbits had no natural predators in Australia.

6. A major reason that humans can have such a significant impact on an ecological community is that humans

(1) can modify their environment through technology
(2) reproduce faster than most other species
(3) are able to increase the amount of finite resources available
(4) remove large amounts of carbon dioxide from the air

7. In lakes in New York State that are exposed to acid rain, fish populations are declining. This is primarily due to changes in which lake condition?

(1) size                            (3) pH
(2) temperature              (4) location

8. Reproduction in humans usually requires

(1) the process of cloning
(2) mitotic cell division of gametes
(3) gametes with chromosomes that are not paired
(4) the external fertilization of sex cells

9. Blood can be tested to determine the presence of the virus associated with the development of AIDS. This blood test is used directly for

(1) cure                           (3) diagnosis
(2) treatment                (4) prevention

10. Muscle cells in athletes often have more mitochondria than muscle cells in nonathletes. Based on this observation, it can be inferred that the muscle cells in athletes

(1) have a smaller demand for cell proteins than the muscle cells of nonathletes
(2) reproduce less frequently than the muscle cells of nonathletes
(3) have nuclei containing more DNA than nuclei in the muscle cells of nonathletes
(4) have a greater demand for energy than the muscle cells of nonathletes

**Day 7**

**Stop.** Check your answers and note how many correct **Points**

# Day 7                 Answers and Explanations

1. **1**      Receptors are specialized structures on cells that response only to specific stimuli or chemicals such as hormones.

2. **1**      Hereditary information = DNA ( A, C, G & T)
                                        base sequence

3. **2**      "Resistance," is brought about by *changes (mutations)* on genetic codes of certain individuals of a species.

4. **1**      Protein are broken down into amino acids.
            Enzymes, which aid in digestions, are proteins.

5. **4**      Of all the statements given, only Choice 4 will contribute to a large population growth of a species (rabbits).

            Choices 1 and 3 will have opposite effect on the rabbit population. *Eliminate Choices 1 and 3.*

            Choice 2 statement does not apply to rabbits because rabbits reproduce sexually.

6. **1**      Human activities that have significant impact on ecological community include deforestation, building dams, and destruction of habitats of native species.

            These activities are achieved much more easily with the use of technology.

            The more technological advanced humans get, the easier it is to modify and change ecological communities.

7. **3**      Acid rain = measureable by pH level.

    **39**

8. **3**        Reproduction in humans requires sperm and egg cells (gametes)

          Each gamete = half the (unpaired) chromosomes.

9. **3**        Blood testing = diagnosing diseases.

10. **4**       Mitochondria = Energy producing organelle

          Eliminate Choices 2 and 3 since the functions described in these choices are not directly related to energy production.

          Of the two remaining choices, it makes sense to infer that cells of athletes will have more mitochondria than cells of nonathletes since athletes require more energy.

**Start:** Answer all questions on this day before stopping.

1. Which statement best expresses the relationship between the three structures represented below?

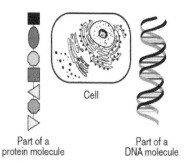

Part of a
protein molecule

Part of a
DNA molecule

Cell

(1) DNA is produced from protein absorbed by the cell.
(2) Protein is composed of DNA that is produced in the cell.
(3) DNA controls the production of protein in the cell.
(4) Cells make DNA by digesting protein.

2. Cellular communication is illustrated in the diagram below.

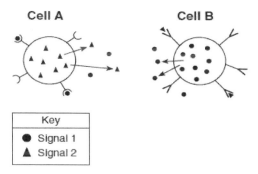

Cell A          Cell B

| Key | |
|---|---|
| ● | Signal 1 |
| ▲ | Signal 2 |

Information can be sent from

(1) cell *A* to cell *B* because cell *B* is able to recognize signal 1
(2) cell *A* to cell *B* because cell *A* is able to recognize signal 2
(3) cell *B* to cell *A* because cell *A* is able to recognize signal 1
(4) cell *B* to cell *A* because cell *B* is able to recognize signal 2

3. The diagram below represents a human reproductive system.

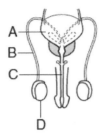

Meiosis occurs within structure

(1) *A*                    (3) *C*
(2) *B*                    (4) *D*

4. The diagram below represents a portion of a type of organic molecule present in the cells of organisms.

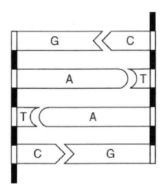

What will most likely happen if there is a change in the base sequence of this molecule?

(1) The molecule will be converted into an inorganic compound.
(2) The amino acid sequence may be altered during protein synthesis.
(3) The chromosome number will decrease in future generations.
(4) The chromosome number may increase within the organisms.

5. The diagram below represents an autotrophic cell.

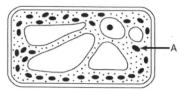

For the process of autotrophic nutrition, the arrow labeled *A* would most likely represent the direction of movement of

(1) carbon dioxide, water, and solar energy
(2) oxygen, glucose, and solar energy
(3) carbon dioxide, oxygen, and heat energy
(4) glucose, water, and heat energy

6. A pond ecosystem is shown in the diagram below.

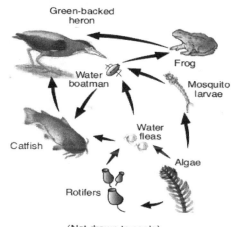

(Not drawn to scale)

Which statement describes an interaction that helps maintain the dynamic equilibrium of this ecosystem?

(1) The frogs make energy available to this ecosystem through the process of photosynthesis.
(2) The algae directly provide food for both the rotifers and the catfish.
(3) The green-backed heron provides energy for the mosquito larvae.
(4) The catfish population helps control the populations of water boatman and water fleas.

7. Which model best represents the relationship between a cell, a nucleus, a gene, and a chromosome?

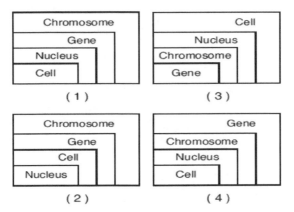

8. The diagram below shows how a coverslip should be lowered onto some single-celled organisms during the preparation of a wet mount.

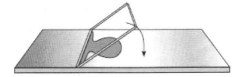

Why is this a preferred procedure?

(1) The coverslip will prevent the slide from breaking.
(2) The organisms will be more evenly distributed.
(3) The possibility of breaking the coverslip is reduced.
(4) The possibility of trapping air bubbles is reduced.

9. The chart below contains both autotrophic and heterotrophic organisms

| A | owl | cat | shark |
| --- | --- | --- | --- |
| B | mouse | corn | dog |
| C | squirrel | bluebird | alga |

Organisms that carry out only heterotrophic nutrition are found in

(1) row *A*, only                    (3) rows *A* and *B*
(2) row *B*, only                    (4) rows *A* and *C*

10. An ecosystem is represented below.

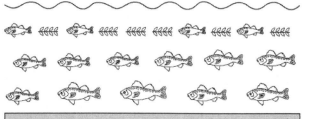 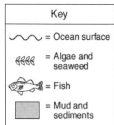

The organisms represented as  are found in the area shown due to which factor?

(1) pH                               (3) light intensity
(2) sediment                      (4) colder temperature

**Day 8**

**Stop.** Check your answers and note how many correct **Points**

1. **3**      *The b*ase sequence of a DNA molecule determines which amino acid is synthesized.

               Proteins are made by joining amino acids together in the cell.

               DNA, therefore, controls the production of protein.

2. **3**      *Based on the cell diagrams:*
               Cell B produces Signal 1
               Cell A contains receptors that are specific to Signal 1

               Information (Signal 1 from B) can be sent to Cell A because A contains receptors to recognize Signal 1.

3. **4**      Meiosis = Produce monoploids (sperms) in testicles (D)

               A is the bladder (collects and stores urine).
               B is the vas deferens (carries sperm)
               C is the urethra (carries urine)

4. **2**      The portion of the molecule given in the diagram is of a DNA, which codes for amino acids

               Changes in DNA sequence = Changes in amino acid sequence.

5. **1**      The cell shown represents that of a plant (an autotroph) .

               Arrow A shows movement into what appears to be chloroplast (photosynthesis organelle in autotrophs).

               Arrow A likely represents movement of materials needed for photosynthesis: *carbon dioxide, water, and solar energy.*

6. **4**      *Dynamic equilibrium* is maintained in an ecosystem when the populations of the species are well controlled.

               Choice 4 is the best answer because it deals with population control of the species of that ecosystem

7. **3**          Genes are found on chromosomes.
                  Chromosomes are found in the nucleus
                  Nucleus is an organelle of the cell.

                  Choice 3 diagram correctly represents this level of organization.

8. **4**          Lowering the coverslip as shown allows air to be pushed out
                  as the coverslip makes contact with the wet mount on the slide.

                  This reduces the likelihood of trapping bubbles between the
                  coverslip and the slide.

9. **1**          Autotrophs   =   make their own materials for energy.
                  Autotrophs   =   plants, algae, and some bacteria.

                  Heterotrophs =   break down carbohydrates for energy
                  Heterotrophs =   all species in the animal kingdom.

                  On the data table, only Group A contains just heterotrophic
                  (*animal kingdom*) organisms.

10. **3**         According to diagram , organism 🌿 represents algae

                  and seaweed, which are autotrophic organisms.

                  These organisms require sunlight to produce their own
                  organic materials through photosynthesis.

                  They are found just beneath the ocean surface because *light
                  intensity* from the sun will be very strong near the surface.

**Start:** Answer all questions on this day before stopping.

1. Complete the chart below by identifying *two* cell structures involved in protein synthesis and stating how *each* structure functions in protein synthesis. [2]

| Cell Structure | Function in Protein Synthesis |
|---|---|
|  |  |
|  |  |

2. The graphs below show dissolved oxygen content, sewage waste content, and fish populations in a lake between 1950 and 1970.

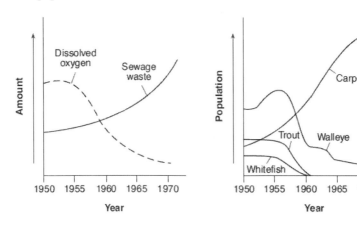

State what happened to the amount of dissolved oxygen and the number of fish species as the amount of sewage waste increased. [1]

_____

_____

3. To prevent harm to the fetus, women should avoid tobacco, alcohol, and certain medications during pregnancy. State *one* specific way that *one* of these substances could harm the fetus. [1]

_____

4. Write the structures listed below in order from least complex to most
   complex. [1]

> organ
> cell
> organism
> organelle
> tissue

Least complex: _____

_____

↓ _____

_____

Most complex: _____

*Base your answers to questions 5 and 6 on the information below and on your
knowledge of biology.*

> The hedgehog, a small mammal native to Africa and Europe, has
> been introduced to the United States as an exotic pet species.
> Scientists have found that hedgehogs can transfer pathogens to
> humans and domestic animals. Foot-and-mouth viruses,
> *Salmonella*, and certain fungi are known pathogens carried by
> hedgehogs. As more and more of these exotic animals are brought
> into this country, the risk of infection increases in the human
> population.

5. State *one negative* effect of importing exotic species to the United States. [1]

_____

_____

6. State *one* way the human immune system might respond to an invading
   pathogen associated with handling a hedgehog. [1]

_____

_____

*Base your answers to questions 7 and 8 on the experimental setup shown below.*

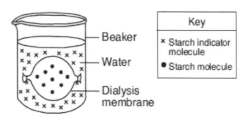

7. On the diagram below, draw in the expected locations of the molecules after a period of one hour. [1]

8. When starch indicator is used, what observation would indicate the presence of starch? [1]

_____

_____

9. A dichotomous key is shown below.

### Dichotomous Key

1. a. tail fins are horizontal.................go to 2
   b. tail fins are vertical....................go to 3

2. a. has teeth or tusk.......................go to 4
   b. has no teeth............................**Balaena mysticetus**

3. a. has gill slits behind mouth............go to 5
   b. has no gill slits.........................**Lepidosiren paradoxa**

4. a. black with white underside............**Orcinus orca**
   b. tusk, gray with dark spots.............**Monodon monoceros**

5. a. head is hammer shaped...............**Sphyrna mokarran**
   b. tail fins are half the body length......**Alopias vulpinus**

Use the dichotomous key to identify the scientific name of the organism represented below. [1]

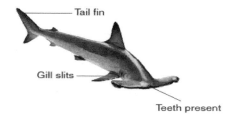

Tail fin

Gill slits

Teeth present

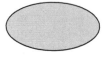

### Day 9

**Stop.** Check your answers and note how many correct **Points**

**1. 2 points**     **Your response will vary from those listed below. However, allow points based on the followings.**

**1 point** for correctly identifying a cell structure AND correctly stating its function in protein synthesis.

**1 point** for doing the same for a second cell structure with a different function in protein synthesis.

**Acceptable 2-point responses include, but are not limited to:**

*nucleus* – *contains template, code, or instructions for protein synthesis*

*ribosome* – *assembles proteins; synthesizes proteins*

*mitochondrion* – *provides energy*

**2. 1 point**     **According to the first graph:**
As the amount of sewage waste increases, the amount of dissolved oxygen decreases.

**According to the second graph**
There is a decline in population for three of the four species of fish during the same time the sewage waste increases.

**Acceptable response include, but are not limited to:**

*Both the dissolved oxygen amount and the number of fish species decrease as sewage waste increases*

**3. 1 point**     **Acceptable responses include, but are not limited to:**

*interfere with development*

*cause low birth weight*

*cause death of the fetus*

*cause Fetal Alcohol Syndrome*

**NOTE:** Your response MUST be specific.
No point should be credited for just stating that the "fetus will be harmed or hurt."

**4. 1 point**     *Only* the order listed below is an acceptable response.

Least Complex:   *organelle*
                 *tissue*
                 *cell*
                 *organ*
Most Complex:    *organism*

**5. 1 point**     **Acceptable responses include, but are not limited to:**

*They can transfer pathogens to humans and domestic animals.*

*Increase risk of salmonella infection on human and animals*

*Imported species may displace native species.*

*Increased competition for food and/or habitat for native species*

**6. 1 point**     **Acceptable responses include, but are not limited to:**

*Make antibodies*

*Activate white blood cells to surround and destroy pathogens.*

**7. 1 point**     A dialysis membrane will be impermeable to starch because starch molecules are too large. It will be permeable to starch indicator molecules because they are much smaller.

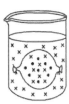

**Acceptable drawing should show:**

All the • 's inside the membrane only,
         and
some of the **x** 's inside and some outside the membrane

| Day 9 | Answers and Explanations |
|---|---|

8. **1 point**   Indicators are substances that change color in the presence of another substance.

**Acceptable responses include, but are not limited to:**

*A blue-black color would indicate the presence of starch.*

*A color change would occur.*

9. **1 point**   *Only* the scientific name below is acceptable .

*Sphyrna mokarran   or   S. mokarran.*

**Start:** Answer all questions on this day before stopping.

1. Which two systems are most directly involved in providing molecules needed for the synthesis of fats in human cells?

   (1) digestive and circulatory
   (2) excretory and digestive
   (3) immune and muscular
   (4) reproductive and circulatory

2. Abiotic factors that characterize a forest ecosystem include

   (1) light and biodiversity
   (2) temperature and amount of available water
   (3) types of producers and decomposers
   (4) pH and number of heterotrophs

3. The presence of some similar structures in all vertebrates suggests that these vertebrates

   (1) all develop at the same rate
   (2) evolved from different animals that appeared on Earth at the same time
   (3) all develop internally and rely on nutrients supplied by the mother
   (4) may have an evolutionary relationship

4. Which statement does *not* describe an example of a feedback mechanism that maintains homeostasis?

   (1) The guard cells close the openings in leaves, preventing excess water loss from a plant.
   (2) White blood cells increase the production of antigens during an allergic reaction.
   (3) Increased physical activity increases heart rate in humans.
   (4) The pancreas releases insulin, helping humans to keep blood sugar levels stable.

5. All chemical breakdown processes in cells directly involve

   (1) reactions that are controlled by catalysts
   (2) enzymes that are stored in mitochondria
   (3) the production of catalysts in vacuoles
   (4) enzymes that have the same genetic base sequence

6. A mutation that can be inherited by offspring would result from

(1) random breakage of chromosomes in the nucleus of liver cells
(2) a base substitution in gametes during meiosis
(3) abnormal lung cells produced by toxins in smoke
(4) ultraviolet radiation damage to skin cells

7. Tissues develop from a zygote as a direct result of the processes of

(1) fertilization and meiosis
(2) fertilization and differentiation
(3) mitosis and meiosis
(4) mitosis and differentiation

8. One advantage of biodiversity in an ecosystem is that it

(1) guarantees that the largest organisms will dominate the area
(2) ensures a large amount of identical genetic material
(3) develops relationships between organisms that are always positive over long periods of time
(4) increases the chance that some organisms will survive a major change in the environment

9. Much of the carbon dioxide produced by green plants is *not* excreted as a metabolic waste because it

(1) can be used for photosynthesis
(2) is too large to pass through cell membranes
(3) is needed for cellular respiration
(4) can be used for the synthesis of proteins

10. Many farmers plant corn, and then harvest the entire plant at the end of the growing season. One *negative* effect of this action is that

(1) soil minerals used by corn plants are not recycled
(2) corn plants remove acidic compounds from the air all season long
(3) corn plants may replace renewable sources of energy
(4) large quantities of water are produced by corn plants

**Day 10**

**Stop.** Check your answers and note how many correct **Points**

# Track Your Progress

If you have completed days 1, 4, 7 and 10 multiple choice question sets, you can easily check your progress and improvements in this question category.

. Go to page 273

. Plot and graph the number of points you got correct on each of the days using the first graph on the page (the 10-point graph).

You hope to see an upward trend on the graph, which indicates improvement and progress.

If you are not satisfied with your performance and progress, it is highly recommended that you study a bit more from your review packets and books before continuing on to the next sets of questions in this book.

1. **1**          Fat synthesis requires glucose, a product of *digestion.*

Cells get glucose from digestion through *circulation.*

2. **2**          Abiotic factor = nonliving or physical condition that affects survival of a species in its ecosystem.

In a forest ecosystem, conditions such as *temperature* and *water* have direct influence on the survival of the forest species (plants, grass..etc)

3. **4**          The key phrase in this question is "similar structure".

Similar structure = related or common evolutionary ancestor

4. **2**          Of all the choices given, the response to allergic reaction described in Choice 2 does not maintain homeostasis.

5. **1**          Chemical breakdown processes = chemical reactions
Catalysts control the speed of these reactions in cells.

6. **2**          Mutation = a result of abnormal information in the base sequence of DNA.

7. **4**          A zygote is formed from fertilization.

*Eliminate Choices 1 and 2* because the question is asking for two processes that change a zygote into tissues (specialized cells).

*Mitosis* divides embryonic cells (zygote) into groups of cells.

*Differentiation* changes the cells into tissue cells that can perform specialized life functions.

8. **4**    Biodiversity = variations (many different kinds) of species in an ecosystem.

Variation = great chance of having a species with a specific characteristic to adapt and survive a changed ennvironment.

9. **1**    Carbon dioxide ($CO_2$) and water ($H_2O$) are the two inorganic reactants needed by plants for photosynthesis.

10. **1**    This question can be answered by just considering which of the choices is a "negative effect."

Only Choice 1 statement indicates a negative effect.

The other three choices indicate positive effects.

Start: Answer all questions on this day before stopping.

1. Which phrase belongs in box *X* of the flowchart below?

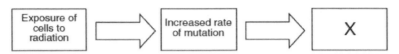

(1) Increased chance of cancer
(2) Increase in the production of functional gametes
(3) Decrease in genetic variability of offspring
(4) Decreased number of altered genes

2. Which graph illustrates changes that indicate a state of dynamic equilibrium in a mosquito population?

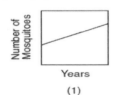

(1)

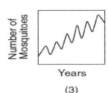

(3)

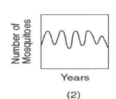

(2)

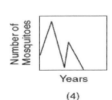

(4)

3. The diagram below shows a cell in the human body engulfing a bacterial cell.

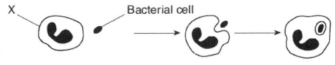

The cell labeled *X* is most likely a

(1) red blood cell
(2) white blood cell

(3) liver cell
(4) nerve cell

4. An energy pyramid is represented below.

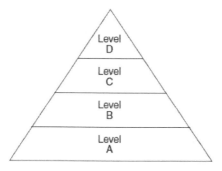

The energy for use by organisms in level *A* originally comes from

(1) producers                          (3) level *B*
(2) the Sun                            (4) level *D*

5. The graph below provides information about the reproductive rates of four species of bacteria, *A*, *B*, *C*, and *D*, at different temperatures.

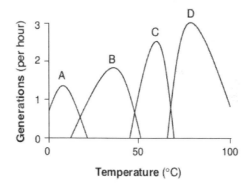

Which statement is a valid conclusion based on the information in the graph?

(1) Changes in temperature cause bacteria to adapt to form new species.
(2) Increasing temperatures speed up bacterial reproduction.
(3) Bacteria can survive only at temperatures between 0°C and 100°C.
(4) Individual species reproduce within a specific range of temperatures.

6. The diagram below represents a plant cell.

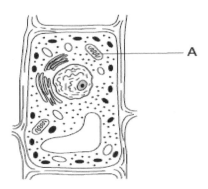

Which process takes place in structure *A*?

(1) cellular respiration              (3) digestion of fats
(2) heterotrophic nutrition           (4) protein synthesis

***Base your answers to questions 7 and 8 on the diagram below, which represents a sequence of events in a biological process that occurs within human cells and on your knowledge of biology.***

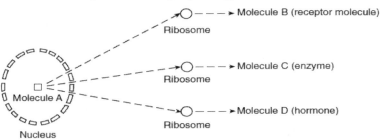

7. Molecule *A* contains the

(1) starch necessary for ribosome synthesis in the cytoplasm
(2) organic substance that is broken down into molecules *B*, *C*, and *D*
(3) proteins that form the ribosome in the cytoplasm
(4) directions for the synthesis of molecules *B*, *C*, and *D*

8. Molecules *B*, *C*, and *D* are similar in that they are usually

(1) composed of genetic information
(2) involved in the synthesis of antibiotics
(3) composed of amino acids
(4) involved in the diffusion of oxygen into the cell

9. Compounds containing phosphorus that are dumped into the environment can upset ecosystems because phosphorus acts as a fertilizer. The graph below shows measurements of phosphorus concentrations taken during the month of June at two sites from 1991 to 1997.

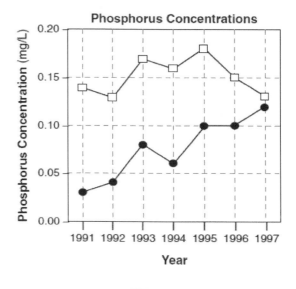

**Phosphorus Concentrations**

Key

Site 1 —□—

Site 2 —●—

Which statement represents a valid inference based on information in the graph?

(1) There was no decrease in the amount of compounds containing phosphorus dumped at site 2 during the period from 1991 to 1997.

(2) Pollution controls may have been put into operation at site 1 in 1995.

(3) There was most likely no vegetation present near site 2 from 1993 to 1994.

(4) There was a greater variation in phosphorous concentration at site 1 than there was at site 2.

10. What is the approximate length of the earthworm shown in the diagram below?

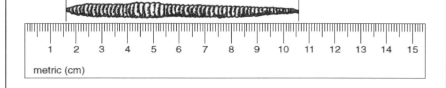

(1) 9 mm

(2) 90 mm

(3) 10.6 cm

(4) 106 cm

**Day 11**

**Stop.** Check your answers and note how many correct **Points**

# Track Your Progress

If you have completed days 2, 5, 8 and 11 multiple choice question sets with graphs, tables, and diagrams, you can easily check your progress and improvements in this question category.

. Go to page 274

. Plot and graph the number of points you got correct on each of the days using the first graph on the page (the 10-point graph).

You hope to see an upward trend on the graph, which indicates improvement and progress.

If you are not satisfied with your performance and progress, it is highly recommended that you study a bit more from your review packets and books before continuing on to the next sets of questions in this book.

1. **1**      Mutation and cancer are related:

Mutation = abnormal changes in gene, chromosome, or cell.

Cancer = rapid and uncontrolled division of a mutation.

Increase rate of mutation = increase chance of cancer.

2. **2**      Equilibrium = a state of stability

Only Choice 2 graph shows mosquito population being kept at a stable number.

3. **2**      A cell in a human body engulfing a bacteria cell is likely a defense (an immune) mechanism.

White blood cells (leukocytes) are immune system cells that response against microorganisms such as bacteria.

4. **2**      In any energy pyramid, the producers are at the bottom (Level A) of the pyramid.

Producers make their own energy through photosynthesis, which requires *sunlight energy.*

5. **4**      According to the graph, the reproductive rate (number of generation per hour) for each of the bacteria species increases, then decreases sharply once a certain temperature is reached.

*Conclusion:* Reproduction rate occurs within a specific temperature range for each species. (Choice 4)

6. **1**      Structure A is the mitochondria.

*Mitochondria (A)* = Cellular respiration (energy making) organelle.

7. **4**        Receptor (B), enzyme (C), and hormone (D) are protein molecules.

Since molecule A is in the nucleus, it likely contains the DNA sequence (direction or genetic code) for joining amino acids together to synthesize proteins B, C and D in the ribosome.

8. **3**        All three are proteins, which are composed of amino acids.

9. **2**        *According to the graph:*

*Between 1991 to 1995, phosphorous concentration at:*
Site 1 = increases

Site 2 = increases

*From 1995 to 1997, phosphorous concentration at:*
Site 1 = decreases (a change likely due to action taken)

Site 2 = increases (no change likely due to no action taken)

10. **2**      The earthworm stretches from 1.6 cm to 10.6 cm.

The length of the worm is the difference between the centimeters:

10.6 cm − 1.6 cm = 9 cm (not a choice)

1 cm = 10 mm

*therefore*

9 cm = *90 mm*

**Start:** Answer all questions on this day before stopping

*Base your answers to questions 1 through 3 on the information below and on your knowledge of biology.*

A park with a small lake is home to a population of ducks. The building of a housing complex eliminates a nearby pond. Soon other ducks and waterbirds like geese and egrets come to live at this small lake.

1. State *one* specific way the new populations of birds may affect the original population of ducks. [1]

_____

_____

2. State *one* specific way the new populations of birds may change the abiotic factors of the environment in and around the lake. [1]

_____

_____

3. Predict *one* way the new populations of birds may affect the populations of plants that live in and around the lake. [1]

_____

_____

4. Data from two different cells are shown in the graphs below.

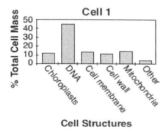
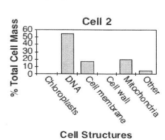

Which cell is most likely a plant cell? Support your answer. [1]

_____

_____

*Base your answers to questions 5 through 8 on the passage below and on your knowledge of biology. The letters indicate paragraphs.*

**Yellow Fever**

**Paragraph A**

     A team of doctors was sent to Havana, Cuba, to study a yellow fever epidemic. The doctors wanted to find out how the pathogenic microbe that causes yellow fever is transferred from those who are sick to those who are well. Some people thought that the disease was spread by having contact with a person who had the disease or even through contact with clothing or bedding that they had used.

**Paragraph B**

     It was known that yellow fever occurred more frequently in swampy environments than in environments that were dry. Consequently, some people thought that the disease was due to contact with the atmosphere of the swamps. A respected doctor in Havana was convinced that a particular species of mosquito, *Aedes calopus,* spread the disease.

**Paragraph C**

     The team of doctors carried out several experiments and collected data. They built poorly ventilated houses in which American soldiers volunteered to sleep on bedding used by individuals who had recently died of yellow fever in local hospitals. The soldiers also wore the nightshirts of those who had died. The houses were fumigated to kill all mosquitoes and the doors and windows of the houses were screened. None of the soldiers living in these houses contracted the disease, though the experiment was tried repeatedly.

**Paragraph D**

     In another experiment, the team built houses that were tightly sealed. The doors and windows were screened. The insides of the houses were divided into two parts by mosquito netting. One part of the house contained a species of mosquito, *Aedes calopus that* had been allowed to bite yellow fever patients in the hospital. There were no mosquitoes in the other part of the house. A group of volunteers lived in each part of the house. A number of those who lived in the part of the house with the mosquitoes became infected; none of those in the other part of the house did.

**Paragraph E**

     Putting these facts together with other evidence, the team concluded that *Aedes calopus* spread the disease. The validity of this conclusion then had to be tested. All newly reported cases of yellow fever were promptly taken to well-screened hospitals and their houses were fumigated to kill any mosquitoes. The breeding places of the mosquitoes in and around Havana were drained or covered with a film of oil to kill mosquito larvae. Native fish species known to feed on mosquito larvae were introduced into streams and ponds. The number of yellow fever cases steadily declined until Havana was essentially free of the epidemic.

5. State the problem the team of doctors was trying to solve. [1]

_____

_____

6. State *one* hypothesis from paragraph *A* that was tested by one of the experiments. [1]

_____

_____

7. Describe the control that should have been set up for the experiment described in paragraph *C*. [1]

_____

_____

8. Explain why the use of native fish (described in paragraph *E*), rather than the use of pesticides, is less likely to have a *negative* impact on the environment. [1]

_____

_____

9. A laboratory setup for a demonstration is represented in the diagram below.

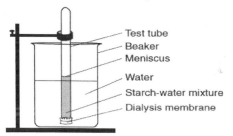

- Test tube
- Beaker
- Meniscus
- Water
- Starch-water mixture
- Dialysis membrane

Describe how an indicator can be used to determine if starch diffuses through the membrane into the beaker. In your answer, be sure to include:
- the procedure used [1]
- how to interpret the results [1]

_____

_____

**Day 12**

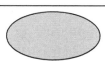

**Stop.** Check your answers and note how many correct **Points**

**Questions 1-3:** The key point in the paragraph has to do with introducing a new species into a stable ecosystem of of another species. Your answers to questions 1 through 3 should reflect this fact.

1. **1 point**     **Acceptable responses include, but are not limited to:**

   *There will be competition for food and space between the new populations of water birds and the original population of ducks.*

   *New individuals of the same species as the original duck population may compete for mates.*

   *New population of water birds may bring disease with them*

   *Original population of ducks may decline*

2. **1 point**     Abiotic factors are the nonliving components of a habitat.

   **Acceptable responses include, but are not limited to:**

   *Bird waste will **pollute the water** and make it cloudy.*

   *Additional waste might **change the pH** of the lake.*

   *New birds will decrease the amount of **space available** to other birds.*

   **NOTE:** Your answer must be a specific abiotic factor.

   Just stating "Pollution" is not an acceptable response

3. **1 point**     Effects on the plant species could be positive or negative.

   **Acceptable responses include, but are not limited to:**

   *More birds will eat the plants, so the plant populations will decrease in number.*

   *Some birds will eat organisms that eat plants. Since there will be fewer primary consumers, the plant populations will increase in number.*

   *Bird wastes will make the soil more fertile so more plants will grow.*

   *The population of plants will decrease.*

4. **1 point**     *Cell 1*

Plant cells have chloroplast and cell wall, unlike animal cells.

According to Cell 1 data, chloroplast and cell wall are present.

5. **1 point**     **Acceptable responses include, but are not limited to:**

*The problem was to determine how the yellow fever microbe was being transferred from person to person.*

*How is yellow fever spread?*

6. **1 point**     **Acceptable responses include, but are not limited to:**

*Yellow fever is spread by contact with the clothing of people who had yellow fever.*

NOTE: Your hypothesis should NOT be stated as a question.

7. **1 point**     **Acceptable responses include, but are not limited to:**

*The control should have been a group of people sleeping in nightshirts or bedding that had not been used by yellow fever patients.*

8. **1 point**     **Acceptable responses include, but are not limited to:**

*Pesticides can harm other parts of the environment (other species) but native fish will not.*

*Native species will target the larvae with less disruption of food chains.*

*Pesticides may disrupt the food chains in the area but native fish will not.*

*Pesticides may cause human illness.*

9. **2 points**    Acceptable 2-point responses include, but not limited to.

**Describing the procedure used (1 point)**

*Add starch indicator solution to the water in the beaker.*

**Describing how to interpret the results  (1 point)**

*If the indicator solution changes color, then starch is present.*

*If indicator solution have no change in color, then no starch is present.*

# Track Your Progress

If you have completed days 3, 6, 9 and 12 short answer question sets, you can easily check your progress and improvements in this question category.
. Go to page 275

. Plot and graph the number of points you got correct on each of the days.

You hope to see an upward trend on the graph, which indicates improvement and progress.

If you are not satisfied with your performance and progress, it is highly recommended that you study a bit more from your review packets and books before continuing on to the next sets of questions in this book.

Start: Answer all questions on this day before stopping

1. A characteristic of a DNA molecule that is *not* characteristic of a protein molecule is that the DNA molecule

(1) can replicate itself
(2) can be very large
(3) is found in nuclei
(4) is composed of subunits

2. A tree produces only seedless oranges. A small branch cut from this tree produces roots after it is planted in soil. When mature, this new tree will most likely produce

(1) oranges with seeds, only
(2) oranges without seeds, only
(3) a majority of oranges with seeds and only a few oranges without seeds
(4) oranges and other kinds of fruit

3. Mutations that occur in skin or lung cells have little effect on the evolution of a species because mutations in these cells

(1) usually lead to the death of the organism
(2) cannot be passed on to offspring
(3) are usually beneficial to the organism
(4) lead to more serious mutations in offspring

4. What will most likely happen to wastes containing nitrogen produced as a result of the breakdown of amino acids within liver cells of a mammal?
(1) They will be digested by enzymes in the stomach.
(2) They will be removed by the excretory system.
(3) They will be destroyed by specialized blood cells.
(4) They will be absorbed by mitochondria in nearby cells.

5. Which two structures of a frog would most likely have the same chromosome number?

(1) skin cell and fertilized egg cell     (3) kidney cell and egg cell
(2) zygote and sperm cell     (4) liver cell and sperm cell

6. In an ecosystem, the growth and survival of organisms are dependent on the availability of the energy from the Sun. This energy is available to organisms in the ecosystem because

(1) producers have the ability to store energy from light in organic molecules
(2) consumers have the ability to transfer chemical energy stored in bonds to plants
(3) all organisms in a food web have the ability to use light energy
(4) all organisms in a food web feed on autotrophs

7. Which change is a cause of the other three?

(1) increased fossil fuel consumption
(2) destruction of the ozone shield
(3) increased industrialization
(4) destruction of natural habitats

8. The sequence of events occurring in the life cycle of a bacterium is listed below.
   (A) The bacterium copies its single chromosome.
   (B) The copies of the chromosome attach to the cell membrane of the bacterium.
   (C) As the cell grows, the two copies of the chromosome separate.
   (D) The cell is separated by a wall into equal halves.
   (E) Each new cell has one copy of the chromosome.

This sequence most closely resembles the process of

(1) recombination
(2) zygote formation
(3) mitotic cell division
(4) meiotic cell division

9. To determine evolutionary relationships between organisms, a comparison would most likely be made between all of the characteristics below *except*

(1) methods of reproduction
(2) number of their ATP molecules
(3) sequences in their DNA molecules
(4) structure of protein molecules present

10. In December 2004, a tsunami (giant wave) destroyed many of the marine organisms along the coast of the Indian Ocean. What can be expected to happen to the ecosystem that was most severely hit by the tsunami?

   (1) The ecosystem will change until a new stable community is established.
   (2) Succession will continue in the ecosystem until one species of marine organism is established.
   (3) Ecological succession will no longer occur in this marine ecosystem.
   (4) The organisms in the ecosystem will become extinct.

11. Which statement describes the reproductive system of a human male?

   (1) It releases sperm that can be used only in external fertilization.
   (2) It synthesizes progesterone that regulates sperm formation
   (3) It produces gametes that transport food for embryo formation.
   (4) It shares some structures with the excretory system.

12. Which process normally occurs at the placenta?

   (1) Oxygen diffuses from fetal blood to maternal blood.
   (2) Materials are exchanged between fetal and maternal blood.
   (3) Maternal blood is converted into fetal blood.
   (4) Digestive enzymes pass from maternal blood to fetal blood.

13. Which result of technological advancement has a positive effect on the environment?

   (1) development of new models of computers each year, with disposal of the old computers in landfills
   (2) development of new models of cars that travel fewer miles per gallon of gasoline
   (3) development of equipment that uses solar energy to charge batteries
   (4) development of equipment to speed up the process of cutting down trees

*Base your answers to questions 14 and 15 on the information below and on your knowledge of biology.*

Organisms living in a bog environment must be able to tolerate nitrogen-poor, acidic conditions. Bog plants such as the Venus flytrap and sundew are able to obtain their nitrogen by attracting and consuming insects. These plants produce chemicals that break down the insects into usable compounds.

14. The chemicals present in the plants that break down the insects are most likely

(1) fats                                  (3) enzymes
(2) hormones                         (4) carbohydrates

15. Which compounds present in insects are composed of the amino acids that provide the Venus flytrap and sundew with much of their nitrogen?

(1) proteins                           (3) carbohydrates
(2) sugars                             (4) fats

**Day 13**

**Stop.** Check your answers and note how many correct **Points**

| **Day 13** | **Answers and Explanations** |
|---|---|

1. **1**    *DNA* = Macromolecule (*large molecule*) in nuclei.

Composed of base sequences (*subunits*).

**Can be replicated.**

*Protein* = Macromolecule (*large molecule*) in nuclei.

Composed of amino acid sequences (*subunits*) .

**Cannot be replicated.**

2. **2**    The tree branch contains the exact same hereditary information for making oranges as the tree itself.

Same hereditary information = same characteristic (oranges without seeds, only)

3. **2**    "Evolution" of a species involves passing on *certain characteristics* from one generation of offsprings to the next.

In this question, it is stated that these mutations "have little effect" on evolution of species.

*Therefore,* it can be concluded that these mutations are not being passed on from one generation to another.

**The other three choices could have been eliminated for the following reasons:**

Choice 1 will have great effects on evolution.

Choice 3 indicates that mutations are beneficial to organisms, which is not true.

Choice 4 will have great effects on evolution.

4. **2**    Waste = not needed = removed through *excretion.*

5. **1**

Full chromosome number $\left\}\right.$ 
Skin cell
Fertilized egg
Zygote
Kidney cell
Liver

Half chromosome number $\left\}\right.$ 
Sperm
Egg   (gametes)

Only choice 1 have two structures from the same set.

6. **1**   The key phrase in this question is "energy from the Sun."

Sun energy is converted to chemical energy by producers (plants) during photosynthesis.

7. **3**   **Negative Effects of Industrialization**

*More fossil fuels* are consumed to maintain industrialization

*Ozone layer* (protective shield against sun radiation) is destroyed because harmful chemicals are released from burning fossil fuels.

*Natural habitats* are destroyed because factories and buildings must be constructed to accommodate industrialization.

8. **3**   The sequence listed = bacterium reproductive cycle

Bacteria reproduce asexually by making identical copies of themselves through mitotic cell division (mitosis) .

9. **2**   The number of ATP molecules varies even within the same organism, and certainly from one organism to another.

*Conclusion:* Comparing number s of ATP molecules will not establish a good evolutionary relationship between organisms.

10. **1**    A disaster like tsunami will most definitely change (but not destroy) an ecosystem.
An ecosystem is changed when most or all of the native organisms no longer live there because of some form of environmental changes (tsunami).

11. **4**    The penis is the part of male reproductive organ that is also involved in the excretory system.

Reproductive organ = path for sperm from male to female

Excretory organ = path for urine removal.

12. **2**    Placenta = connects mom to fetal blood.
Materials (nutrients, oxygen, and wastes) are passed between the mom and fetus through the placenta, only.

13. **3**    *Positive effects from technological advancement on the environment*
. Fewer natural resources used
. Fewer waste and pollution produced

In choice 3: The use of solar energy means no natural resources is used and no waste is produced.

All of the other advancements given will have negative effects on the environment.

14. **3**    The key process being described in the paragraph is digestion (breaking down of food).

Many enzymes (biological catalysts) aid in digestion of food.

15. **1**    Amino acids = building blocks for protein.

Start: Answer all questions on this day before stopping

1. The graph below illustrates the relative amounts of product formed by the action of an enzyme in a solution with a pH of 6 at seven different temperatures.

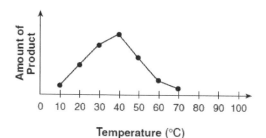

Temperature (°C)

Which statement best expresses the amount of product that will be formed at each temperature if the experiment is repeated at a pH of 4?

(1) The amount of product formed will be equal to that produced at pH 6.
(2) The amount of product formed will be greater than that produced at pH 6.
(3) The amount of product formed will be less than that produced at pH 6.
(4) The amount of product formed can *not* be accurately predicted.

2. The ameba represented in the diagram below is a single-celled organism.

Which two processes are most closely associated with structure *A*?

(1) insertion and deletion
(2) nervous regulation and circulation
(3) active transport and diffusion
(4) replication and photosynthesis

3. The diagram below represents a structure involved in cellular respiration.

Mitochondrion

The release of which substance is represented by the arrows?

(1) glucose                          (3) carbon dioxide
(2) oxygen                           (4) DNA


4. A food web is represented below. Which statement best describes energy in this food web?

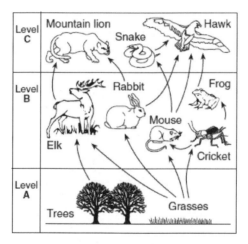

(1) The energy content of level *B* depends on the energy content of level *C*.
(2) The energy content of level *A* depends on energy provided from an abiotic source.
(3) The energy content of level *C* is greater than the energy content of level *A*.
(4) The energy content of level *B* is transferred to level *A*.

5. The development of an embryo is represented in the diagram below.

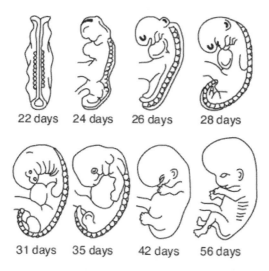

22 days  24 days  26 days  28 days

31 days  35 days  42 days  56 days

(Not drawn to scale)

These changes in the form of the embryo are a direct result of

(1) uncontrolled cell division and mutations
(2) differentiation and growth
(3) antibodies and antigens inherited from the father
(4) meiosis and fertilization

6.The diagram below represents the human female reproductive system.

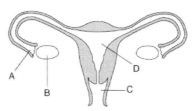

Exposure to radiation or certain chemicals could alter the genetic information in the gametes that form in structure

(1) *A*                                    (3) *C*
(2) *B*                                    (4) *D*

**85**

7. The diagram below represents a species of bee that helps one type of orchid plant reproduce by carrying pollen on structure $X$ from one orchid flower to another. Pollination by this species of bee is the only way the orchid can reproduce.

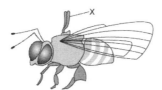

If this bee species dies out, this orchid species would most likely

(1) cease to exist
(2) find another animal to carry the pollen
(3) flower at a different time of year
(4) develop another way to reproduce

8. The diagram below represents a nucleus containing the normal chromosome number for a species.

Which diagram bests illustrates the normal formation of a cell that contains all of the genetic information needed for growth, development, and future reproduction of this species?

9. Some human body structures are represented in the diagram below.

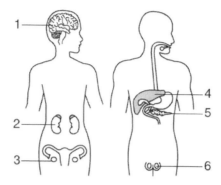

In which structures would the occurrence of mutations have the greatest effect on human evolution?

(1) 1 and 3                    (3) 3 and 6
(2) 2 and 5                    (4) 4 and 6

10. The relative amount of oxygen in the atmosphere of Earth over millions of years is shown in the graph below.

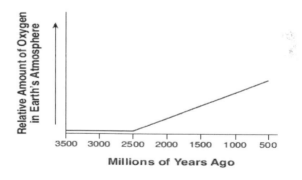

At what point in the history of Earth did autotrophs most likely first appear?

(1) 3500 million years ago          (3) 1500 million years ago
(2) 2500 million years ago          (4) 500 million years ago

11. A food web is represented in the diagram below.

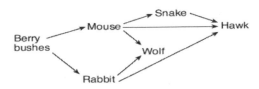

Which population in this food web would most likely be *negatively* affected by an increase in the mouse population?

(1) snake
(2) rabbit

(3) wolf
(4) hawk

12. A biologist collected the data shown in the table below.

**Data Table**

| Type of Organism | Number of Organisms in a Field | | |
|---|---|---|---|
| | May | July | September |
| grasshoppers | 100 | 500 | 150 |
| birds | 25 | 100 | 10 |
| spiders | 75 | 200 | 50 |

Which statement is supported by the data in the table?

(1) Populations do not vary from month to month.
(2) The populations are highest in September.
(3) The grasshoppers increased in length in July.
(4) Seasonal variations may affect populations.

13. The data in the graph below show evidence of disease in the human body.

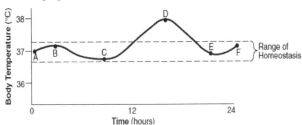

A disruption in dynamic equilibrium is indicated by the temperature change between points

(1) *A* and *B*
(2) *B* and *C*

(3) *C* and *D*
(4) *E* and *F*

14. A classification system is shown in the table below.

| Classification | Examples |
|---|---|
| Kingdom — animal | △, ○, ◻, ☆, ◻, ◇, ⟆, ▽ |
| Phylum — chordata | △, ◻, ⟆, ☆, ◻ |
| Genus — *Felis* | ◻, ⟆ |
| Species — *domestica* | ◻ |

This classification scheme indicates that ☐ is most closely related to

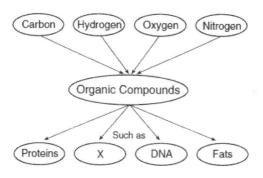

( 1 )     ( 2 )     ( 3 )     ( 4 )

15. What substance could be represented by the letter *X* in the diagram below?

Carbon   Hydrogen   Oxygen   Nitrogen

Organic Compounds

Such as

Proteins   X   DNA   Fats

(1) carbohydrates          (3) carbon dioxide
(2) ozone                   (4) water

**Day 14**

**Stop.** Check your answers and note how many correct **Points**

1. **4**      There is no information in the question or on the graph that can be used to predict the amount of products at pH 4.

2. **3**      Structure A = cell membrane of the amoeba.

   Materials enter and exit a cell by *active transport* and *diffusion* through the cell membrane.

3. **3**      Cellular respiration (shown below) occurs in the mitochondria.

   glucose + oxygen → carbon dioxide + water.

   The arrows likely represent the release of the metabolic waste, carbon dioxide.

4. **2**      The true statement relating to energy in the food web given can be chosen by carefully going through each choice, and eliminating those that are clearly false based on the diagram.

   Choice 2 is the only correct statement because organisms in Level A are the producers, and producers make their energy using *sunlight , an abiotic (a nonliving) factor.*

5. **2**      The embryo is changing (differentiating) and growing over time.

6. **2**      Female gamete = egg cell = forms in the ovary (B)

7. **1**      As stated in the question, the bee species *"is the only way for the orchid to reproduce"*

   Bee species dies = orchid can't reproduce = cease to exist

8. **3**            *The correct diagram must show:*

The two gametes (left of the arrow) containing identical halves of the normal chromosome number.

The cell that forms (right of the arrow) must be exactly the same (contains normal chromosome number) as the one pictured in the question.

Only in Choice 3 are these the case.

9. **3**            A characteristic such as mutation will have an impact on the evolution of a species if the mutation can be passed on from generation to generation.

Structure 3 and 6 are the reproductive organs, which are involved in transmitting (passing on) genetic characteristics of parents to offsprings.

10. **2**            Autotrophs convert carbon dioxide and water into oxygen and glucose during photosynthesis processes.

$$CO_2 \;+\; H_2O \;\rightarrow\; O_2 \;+\; C_6H_{12}O_6$$

The point in history (2500 million years ago) that the relative amount of oxygen starts to increase is likely the first time autotrophs first appear, and start making oxygen.

11. **2**            A population increase of one species will affect another species if both species eat (compete) for the same food.

*According the food web diagram:*

Both the mouse and rabbit eat berry bushes.

Increase mouse population = fewer berry bushes for rabbits.
                                    ( a negative effect)

12. **4**      The data table shows populations of three species for three months from different seasons.

Choice 1:    False. Populations vary from month to month.

Choice 2:    False. Population is highest in September.

Choice 3:    Length measurements is NOT given on the table.

*Choice 4 :   True.  Populations of the three species are different in all three seasons.*

13. **3**      A disruptive in equilibrium = out of range of homeostasis

This occurs between points C and D.

14. **4**      Species in the same genus are very closely related.

Only ⧯ belongs in the same genus as ☐

15. **1**      X must be an organic compound (carbohydrate).

All others are inorganic compounds.

Start: Answer all questions on this day before stopping

*Base your answers to questions 1 through 4 on the passage below and on your knowledge of biology.*

### Decline of the Salmon Population

Salmon are fish that hatch in a river and swim to the ocean where their body mass increases. When mature, they return to the river where they were hatched and swim up stream to reproduce and die. When there are large populations of salmon, the return of nutrients to the river ecosystem can be huge. It is estimated that during salmon runs in the Pacific Northwest in the 1800s, 500 million pounds of salmon returned to reproduce and die each year. Research estimates that in the Columbia River alone, salmon contributed hundreds of thousands of pounds of nitrogen and phosphorus compounds to the local ecosystem each year. Over the past 100 years, commercial ocean fishing has removed up to two-thirds of the salmon before they reach the river each year.

1. Identify the process that releases the nutrients from the bodies of the dead salmon, making the nutrients available for other organisms in the ecosystem. [1]

   _____

2. Identify *one* organism, other than the salmon, that would be present in or near the river that would most likely be part of a food web in the river ecosystem. [1]

   _____

3. Identify *two* nutrients that are returned to the ecosystem when the salmon die. [1]

   _____

   _____

4. State *one* impact, other than reducing the salmon population, that commercial ocean fishing has on the river ecosystem. [1]

   _____

*Base your answers to questions 5 through 7 on the information below and on your knowledge of biology.*

        Scientists found members of a plant species they did not recognize. They wanted to determine if the unknown species was related to one or more of four known species, *A, B, C,* and *D.*

        The relationship between species can be determined most accurately by comparing the results of gel electrophoresis of the DNA from different species.

        The chart below represents the results of gel electrophoresis of the DNA from the unknown plant species and the four known species.

Results of Gel Electrophoresis of DNA from Five Plant Species

Key
——— = Band in the gel

5. The unknown species is most closely related to which of the four known species?
   Support your answer. [1]

   _____

   _____

6. Identify *one* physical characteristic of plants that can be readily observed and compared to help determine the relationship between two different species of plants. [1]

   _____

7. Explain why comparing the DNA of the unknown and known plant species is probably a more accurate method of determining relationships than comparing only the physical characteristic you identified in question 6. [1]

   _____

   _____

*Base your answers to questions 8 and 9 on the statement and diagram below and on your knowledge of biology.*

Women are advised to avoid consuming alcoholic beverages during pregnancy.

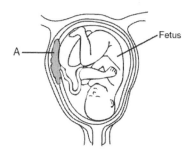

8. Identify the structure labeled *A* and explain how the functioning of structure *A* is essential for the normal development of the fetus. [2]

   Structure *A*: _____

   _____

   _____

   _____

9. Explain why consumption of alcoholic beverages by a pregnant woman is likely to be more harmful to her fetus than to herself. [1]

   _____

   _____

   _____

**Day 15**

**Stop.** Check your answers and note how many correct **Points**

1. **1 point**    **Acceptable responses include, but are not limited to:**

*Decomposition*

*Decay*

*Recycling*

2. **1 point**    **Acceptable responses include, but are not limited to:**

*Decomposer*

*Bacteria*

*Small fish*

*Seagulls*

*Green plant*

3. **1 point**    **Acceptable responses include, but are not limited to:**

*Nitrogen compounds*

*Phosphorus compounds*

*Carbon compounds*

4. **1 point**    **Acceptable responses include, but are not limited to:**

*Fishing deprives upstream ecosystems of nutrients.*

*Consumers in the ecosystem would be deprived of food.*

*Decomposer populations would decrease disrupts food webs*

5. **1 point**    The unknown most closely related to Species C

**Acceptable explanation includes, but is not limited to:**

*The DNA markers (bands) of the unknown has the most match to those of Species C*

# Day 15 Answers and Explanations

**6. 1 point**      **Acceptable responses include, but are not limited to:**

*Structure of flowers*

*Structure of leaves*

*Structure of stems*

*Structure of seeds*

*Structure of pollen*

**7. 1 point**      **Acceptable responses include, but are not limited to:**

*The physical characteristic chosen may be the only characteristic the organisms have in common, while the more similar the DNA, the more characteristics the organisms have in common.*

**8. 2 points**      **Acceptable 2-point responses include, but are not limited to:**

**Identifying structure labeled A (1 points)**

*Placenta*

**Explaining how the functioning of structure *A* is essential for the normal development of the fetus. (1 points)**

*Exchange surface for nutrients or wastes or $O_2$ between mother and fetus*

**9. 1 point**      **Acceptable responses include, but are not limited to:**

*When the alcohol from the mother's bloodstream enters the fetus, the relative amount is much greater due to the smaller size of the fetus.*

*The fetus is still developing.*

Start: Answer all questions on this day before stopping

1. Which organ system in humans is most directly involved in the transport of oxygen?

(1) digestive
(2) nervous
(3) excretory
(4) circulatory

2. When brown tree snakes were accidentally introduced onto the island of Guam, they had no natural predators. These snakes sought out and ate many of the eggs of insect-eating birds. What probably occurred following the introduction of the brown tree snakes?

(1) The bird population increased.
(2) The insect population increased.
(3) The bird population began to seek a new food source.
(4) The insect population began to seek a new food source.

3. The immune system of humans may respond to chemicals on the surface of an invading organism by

(1) releasing hormones that break down these chemicals
(2) synthesizing antibodies that mark these organisms to be destroyed
(3) secreting antibiotics that attach to these organisms
(4) altering a DNA sequence in these organisms

4. What will most likely occur as a result of changes in the frequency of a gene in a particular population?

(1) ecological succession
(2) biological evolution
(3) global warming
(4) resource depletion

5. A scientist is planning to carry out an experiment on the effect of heat on the function of a certain enzyme. Which would *not* be an appropriate first step?

(1) doing research in a library
(2) having discussions with other scientists
(3) completing a data table of expected results
(4) using what is already known about the enzyme

---

6. Kangaroos are mammals that lack a placenta. Therefore, they must have an alternate way of supplying the developing embryo with

(1) nutrients
(2) carbon dioxide
(3) enzymes
(4) genetic information

7. One possible reason for the rise in the average air temperature at Earth's surface is that

(1) decomposers are being destroyed
(2) deforestation has increased the levels of oxygen in the atmosphere
(3) industrialization has increased the amount of carbon dioxide in the air
(4) growing crops is depleting the ozone shield

8. Researchers have found that formaldehyde and asbestos can alter DNA base sequences. Based on this research, the use of these chemicals has been greatly reduced because they

(1) may act as fertilizers, increasing the growth of algae in ponds
(2) have been replaced by more toxic compounds
(3) are capable of causing mutations in humans
(4) interfere with the production of antibiotics by white blood cells

9. Years after the lava from an erupting volcano destroyed an area, grasses started to grow in that area. The grasses were gradually replaced by shrubs, evergreen trees, and finally, by a forest that remained for several hundred years. This entire process is an example of

(1) feedback                    (3) plant preservation
(2) ecological succession       (4) deforestation

10. Which statement best describes a chromosome?

(1) It is a gene that has thousands of different forms.
(2) It has genetic information contained in DNA.
(3) It is a reproductive cell that influences more than one trait.
(4) It contains hundreds of genetically identical DNA molecules.

11. Which cell process occurs only in organisms that reproduce sexually?

(1) mutation                    (3) mitosis
(2) replication                 (4) meiosis

12. The flounder is a species of fish that can live in very cold water. The fish produces an "antifreeze" protein that prevents ice crystals from forming in its blood. The DNA for this protein has been identified. An enzyme is used to cut and remove this section of flounder DNA that is then spliced into the DNA of a strawberry plant. As a result, the plant can now produce a protein that makes it more resistant to the damaging effects of frost. This process is known as

(1) sorting of genes
(2) genetic engineering
(3) recombination of chromosomes
(4) mutation by deletion of genetic material

13. When habitats are destroyed, there are usually fewer niches for animals and plants. This action would most likely *not* lead to a change in the amount of

(1) biodiversity
(2) competition
(3) interaction between species
(4) solar radiation reaching the area

14. Many species of plants interact with harmless underground fungi. The fungi enable the plants to absorb certain essential minerals and the plants provide the fungi with carbohydrates and other nutrients. This describes an interaction between a

(1) parasite and its host
(2) predator and its prey
(3) scavenger and a decomposer
(4) producer and a consumer

15. Which structures carry out life functions within cells?
(1) tissues                              (3) organelles
(2) organ systems                  (4) organs

**Day 16**

**Stop.** Check your answers and note how many correct **Points**

1. **4**        Oxygen is carried by the blood, a key component of the circulatory system

2. **2**        Snakes eat the eggs of insect-eating birds
   - Fewer offsprings of the birds will be produced
   - Fewer insects will be eaten.
     - Insect population will increase.

3. **2**        Immune system = makes antibodies against foreign organisms

4. **2**        "Gene" = biological
   Changes in the frequency of a gene = Biological evolution

5. **3**        A data table should only be completed if results of an experiment are available.
   Collecting results is never a first step in a scientific experiment.

6. **1**        Placenta = connection between embryo to the mother
                   = transports nutrients from mom to the embryo.
   Lack of placenta means there is an alternate way that nutrients are transported from a kangaroos mom to her embryo.

7. **3**        An increase in earth's surface temperature is likely due to heat from the sun being trapped by certain chemicals in the atmosphere.
   Carbon dioxide in the atmosphere can trap heat from the sun, and causes greenhouse effect.

**8. 3**      *Alter DNA base sequence* = Mutation

**9. 2**      The question is describing how one species of a plant replaces another over a period of time.

Ecological succession = a change in the species structure of an ecological community over time.

**10. 2**      Chromosome = organized structure of DNA, which contains genetic information.

**11. 4**      Sexual reproduction = joining of gametes (sperm and egg cells).

Gametes = products of meiosis.

All the other processes listed occur in both sexually and asexually reproduce organisms.

**12. 2**      The process described in the question involves removing a DNA segment from one organism, and putting it into a DNA segment of another organism.

This method is often used in genetic engineering.

**13. 4**      Biodiversity (1), competition (2), and interaction between species (3) are all characteristics of a habitat, and will be changed if a habitat is destroyed.

Solar radiation reaching a habitat *will not* change if the habitat is destroyed.

**14. 4**      The interactions described in the question indicate that both the fungi and the plant species are benefiting from each other because each ***produces*** the essential nutrients that the other ***consumes.***

**15. 3**      The key words in this question is "within cells"

Organelles = Structures within (inside) a cell.

Start: Answer all questions on this day before stopping

1. The arrows in the diagram below indicate the movement of materials into and out of a single celled organism.

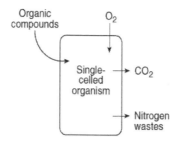

The movements indicated by all the arrows are directly involved in
(1) the maintenance of homeostasis
(2) respiration, only
(3) excretion, only
(4) the digestion of proteins

2. A current proposal in the field of classification divides life into three broad categories called domains. This idea is illustrated below.

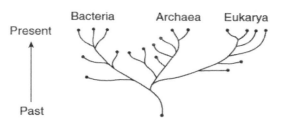

Which concept is best supported by this diagram?
(1) Evolutionary pathways proceed only in one set direction over a short period of time.
(2) All evolutionary pathways will eventually lead to present-day organisms.
(3) All evolutionary pathways are the same length and they all lead to present-day organisms.
(4) Evolutionary pathways can proceed in several directions with only some pathways leading to present-day organisms.

3. Which concept is best illustrated in the flowchart below?

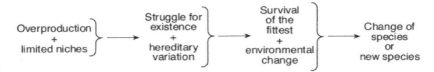

(1) natural selection                          (3) dynamic equilibrium
(2) genetic manipulation                     (4) material cycles

4. The molecule represented below is found in living things.

Which statement describes one characteristic of this molecule?

(1) It is the template for the replication of genetic information.
(2) Organic catalysts are made up of these molecules.
(3) It is different in each cell of an organism.
(4) Cell membranes contain many of these molecules.

5. The diagram below represents a yeast cell that is in the process of budding, a form of asexual reproduction.

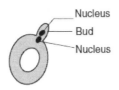

Which statement describes the outcome of this process?

(1) The bud will develop into a zygote.
(2) The two cells that result will each contain half the species number of chromosomes.
(3) The two cells that result will have identical DNA.
(4) The bud will start to divide by the process of meiotic cell division.

---

6. Some organs of the human body are represented in the diagram below.

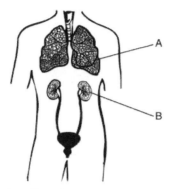

Which statement best describes the functions of these organs?

(1) *B* pumps blood to *A* for gas exchange.

(2) *A* and *B* both produce carbon dioxide, which provides nutrients for other body parts.

(3) *A* releases antibodies in response to an infection in *B*.

(4) The removal of wastes from both *A* and *B* involves the use of energy from ATP.

7. Bacteria that are removed from the human intestine are genetically engineered to feed on organic pollutants in the environment and convert them into harmless inorganic compounds. Which row in the table below best represents the most likely negative and positive effects of this technology on the ecosystem?

| Row | Negative Effect | Positive Effect |
|-----|-----------------|-----------------|
| (1) | Inorganic compounds interfere with cycles in the environment. | Human bacteria are added to the environment. |
| (2) | Engineered bacteria may out-compete native bacteria. | The organic pollutants are removed. |
| (3) | Only some of the pollutants are removed. | Bacteria will make more organic pollutants. |
| (4) | The bacteria will cause diseases in humans. | The inorganic compounds are buried in the soil. |

8. An energy pyramid is represented below.

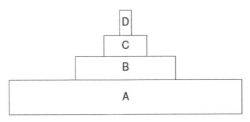

How much energy would be available to the organisms in level *C*?

(1) all of the energy in level *A*, plus the energy in level *B*
(2) all of the energy in level *A*, minus the energy in level *B*
(3) a percentage of the energy contained in level *B*
(4) a percentage of the energy synthesized in level *B* and level *D*

9. A technique used to reproduce plants is shown in the diagram below.

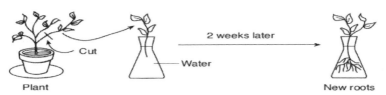

This technique is a form of

(1) sexual reproduction                    (3) gamete production
(2) asexual reproduction                   (4) gene manipulation

10. Which diagram best illustrates the relationship between humans (*H*) and ecosystems (*E*)?

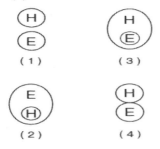

11. In the diagram below, the dark dots indicate small molecules. These molecules are moving out of the cells, as indicated by the arrows. The number of dots inside and outside of the two cells represents the relative concentrations of the molecules inside and outside of the cells.

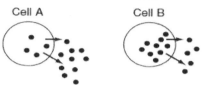

ATP is being used to move the molecules out of the cell by

(1) cell *A*, only

(2) cell *B*, only

(3) both cell *A* and cell *B*

(4) neither cell *A* nor cell *B*

12. The graph below represents data obtained from an experiment on starch digestion.

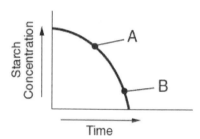

Which statement best describes point *A* and point *B* on the graph?

(1) The concentration of sugars is greater at point *A* than it is at point *B*.

(2) The concentration of sugars is greater at point *B* than it is at point *A*.

(3) The starch concentration is the same at point *A* as it is at point *B*.

(4) The starch concentration is greater at point *B* than it is at point *A*.

13.The diagram below represents two cells, $X$ and $Y$.

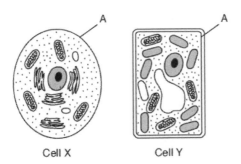

Cell X                    Cell Y

Which statement is correct concerning the structure labeled $A$?

(1) It aids in the removal of metabolic wastes in both cell $X$ and cell $Y$.
(2) It is involved in cell communication in cell $X$, but not in cell $Y$.
(3) It prevents the absorption of $CO_2$ in cell $X$ and $O_2$ in cell $Y$.
(4) It represents the cell wall in cell $X$ and the cell membrane in cell $Y$.

14. The graph below shows photosynthetic activity in an ecosystem over a 24-hour period.

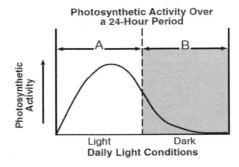

Data for a study on respiration in this ecosystem should be collected during

(1) interval $A$, from only the producers in the ecosystem
(2) intervals $A$ and $B$, from only the consumers in the ecosystem
(3) intervals $A$ and $B$, from both the producers and consumers in the ecosystem
(4) interval $A$ only, from abiotic but not biotic components of the ecosystem

15. An experimental setup is shown in the diagram below.

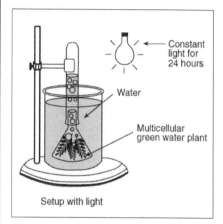 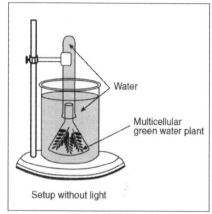

Which hypothesis would most likely be tested using this setup?

(1) Green water plants release a gas in the presence of light.
(2) Roots of water plants absorb minerals in the absence of light.
(3) Green plants need light for cell division.
(4) Plants grow best in the absence of light.

**Day 17**

**Stop.** Check your answers and note how many correct **Points**

1. **1**     Substances going into the cell = needed for cellular respiration.

Substances going out of the cell = excreted wastes

Homeostasis is a process of maintaining stability within an organism through the coordination of many life functions (respiration and excretion in the diagram shown)

2. **4**     According to the pathway diagram, some pathways stop branching off somewhere between the past and present, while other pathways continue to branch off to produce organisms that are still present today.

3. **1**     The key information indicated in the diagram is "survival of the fittest"

Survival of the Fittest = Theory of Natural Selection (Darwin).

4. **1**     A double-helix molecule = DNA.

DNA contains replicable genetic information of an organism.

5. **3**     Asexually reproduction = Offsprings with full chromosome number and identical genetic information (DNA) as the parent cell.

6. **4**     A is the lung = $CO_2$ (a cellular respiration waste) removal.

B is the kidney = urine (a metabolic waste) removal.

All waste removal requires the use of energy (ATP).

7. **2**     Introducing a new (genetically superior) species into a population has a negative effect on the native population.

Organic pollutants are harmful to human, removing them is a positive effect.

8. **3**         Most of the energy produced by organisms at any level of
                 a food chain are used up by those organisms.
                 That means some amount (*percentage*) of the energy
                 is passed on to organisms at the next level of the food chain.

9. **2**         The diagram shows a small piece of the plant growing to
                 a full plant without the joining of two gametes.

                 Gametes not involved  =  asexual reproduction (mitosis)

                 The cut plant piece is able to grow into a full plant by
                 mitotic cell division and differentiation.

10. **2**        An ecosystem includes animal and plant populations
                 interacting within a nonliving environment.

                 Humans are, therefore, part of an ecosystem

                 Choice 2 diagram is the only one showing human being
                 part of (or within) an ecosystem.

11. **1**        Molecules can move across a cell membrane by:

                 Active transport:  uses ATP, and is faster

                 Diffusion: No ATP is used, and is slower.

                 The dark molecules are transported out faster from Cell A
                 than from Cell B because ATP is likely being used in Cell A.

12. **2**       When starch is digested, it is broken down into sugar.

The graph is showing the amount of starch left undigested over time.

Point A = high starch concentration = low sugar concentration

Point B = low starch concentration = high sugar concentration

13. **1**       In both cells X and Y, A is the cell membrane.

cell membrane = contains receptors = cell communication

14. **3**       Cellular respiration (the process of making energy) is a life function carried out by all organisms at any time of the day.

*Therefore:* Accurate study of respiration in this ecosystem should include data collected from both producers and consumers, during interval A (light) and interval B (dark).

15. **1**       The only difference between the two setups is the presence of gas bubbles in the test tube of the setup with light.

Start: Answer all questions on this day before stopping

*Base your answers to questions 1 through 5 on the information below and on your knowledge of biology.*

The average level of carbon dioxide in the atmosphere has been measured for the past several decades. The data collected are shown in the table below.

**Average $CO_2$ Levels in the Atmosphere**

| Year | $CO_2$ (in parts per million) |
|------|-------------------------------|
| 1960 | 320 |
| 1970 | 332 |
| 1980 | 350 |
| 1990 | 361 |
| 2000 | 370 |

*Directions* (1 and 2): Using the information in the data table, construct a line graph on the grid below.

1 Mark an appropriate scale on each labeled axis. [1]

2 Plot the data on the grid. Surround each point with a small circle and connect the points. [1]

Example:

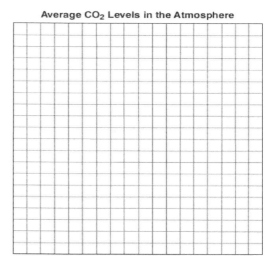

Average $CO_2$ Levels in the Atmosphere

CO₂ (parts per million)

Year

3. Identify *one* specific human activity that could be responsible for the change in carbon dioxide levels from 1960 to 2000. [1]

_____

_____

4. State *one* possible *negative* effect this change in $CO_2$ level has had on the environment of Earth. [1]

_____

_____

5. Calculate the net change in $CO_2$ level in parts per million (ppm) during the years 1960 through 2000. [1]

_____ **ppm**

The human female reproductive system is represented in the diagram below.

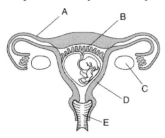

Complete boxes 6 through 9 in the chart below using the information from the diagram. [4]

| Name of Structure | Letter on Diagram | Function of Structure |
|---|---|---|
| 6 _____ | 7 _____ | produces gametes |
| uterus | D | 8 _____ |
| 9 _____ | B | transports oxygen directly to the embryo |

*Base your answer to question 10 on the information and data table below and on your knowledge of biology.*

**Body Structures and Reproductive Characteristics of Four Organisms**

| Organism | Body Structures | Reproductive Characteristics |
|---|---|---|
| pigeon | feathers, scales<br>2 wings, 2 legs | lays eggs |
| A | scales<br>4 legs | lays eggs |
| B | fur<br>2 leathery wings, 2 legs | gives birth to live young<br>provides milk for offspring |
| C | fur<br>4 legs | lays eggs<br>provides milk for offspring |

10. Explain why it would be difficult to determine which one of the other three organisms from the table should be placed in box 1. [1]

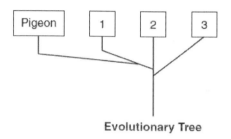

Evolutionary Tree

_____

_____

_____

**Day 18**

**Stop.** Check your answers and note how many correct **Points**

1. 1 point      **For marking appropriate scale each axis.**

2. 1 point      **For appropriate plot and graph**

**Example of a 2-credit graph for questions 1 and 2**

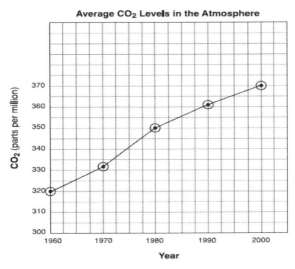

Average $CO_2$ Levels in the Atmosphere

3. 1 point      **Acceptable responses include, but are not limited to:**
   *Increased burning of fossil fuels*
   *More motor vehicle use*
   *Increased levels of deforestation*
   *Increase in human population*

4. 1 point      **Acceptable responses include, but are not limited to:**
   *An increase in the number of severe storms*
   *An increase in sea levels*
   *Flooding of coastal areas*
   *Changes in precipitation patterns*
   *Global warming*
   *Temperature increases*

5. 1 point      *50 ppm    (370 - 320)*

6. **1 point**     *Ovary*

7. **1 point**     *C*

8. **1 point**     **Acceptable responses include, but are not limited to:**
      *Embryonic development*
      *Fetus development*

9. **1 point**     *Placenta*

10. **1 point**     **Acceptable responses include, but are not limited to:**
      *The pigeon shares characteristics with all of the other organisms.*
      *Organisms A and C also lay eggs.*

Start: Answer all questions on this day before stopping

1. In 1910, Thomas Morgan discovered a certain pattern of inheritance in fruit flies known as sex linkage. This discovery extended the ideas of inheritance that Gregor Mendel had discovered while working with garden peas in 1865. Which principle of scientific inquiry does this illustrate?

(1) A control group must be part of a valid experiment.
(2) Scientific explanations can be modified as new evidence is found.
(3) The same experiment must be repeated many times to validate the results.
(4) Values can be used to make ethical decisions about scientific discovery.

2. Which statement best explains the fact that some identical twins appear different from one another?

(1) Their DNA is essentially the same and the environment plays little or no role in the expression of their genes.
(2) Their DNA is very different and the environment plays a significant role in the expression of their genes.
(3) Their DNA is very different and the environment plays little or no role in the expression of their genes.
(4) Their DNA is essentially the same and the environment plays a significant role in the expression of their genes.

3. The transfer of genes from parents to their offspring is known as

(1) differentiation
(2) heredity
(3) immunity
(4) evolution

4. A piece of refrigerated, cooked meat will remain safe to eat for a longer period of time than a refrigerated piece of raw meat of similar size. Which statement is a valid inference based on this information?

(1) Cooking meat kills many bacteria and fungi.
(2) Cool temperatures stimulate the growth of microbes on raw meat.
(3) Raw meat cannot be preserved.
(4) Cooked meat contains antibodies that destroy decomposers.

5. In what way are photosynthesis and cellular respiration similar?

(1) They both occur in chloroplasts.
(2) They both require sunlight.
(3) They both involve organic and inorganic molecules.
(4) They both require oxygen and produce carbon dioxide.

6. When antibiotics were first developed, most infectious diseases could be controlled by them. Today, certain bacteria are resistant to many antibiotics. One possible explanation for this change is that

(1) the antibiotics killed most of the bacteria that did not have a genetic variation for resistance
(2) the bacteria needed to change in order to produce more antibiotics
(3) some of the bacteria learned how to resist the antibiotics
(4) antibiotics have become weaker over the years

7. Which substance usually passes in the greatest amount through the placenta from the blood of the fetus to the blood of the mother?

(1) oxygen                          (3) amino acids
(2) carbon dioxide                  (4) glucose

8. An enzyme known as rubisco enables plants to use large amounts of carbon dioxide. This enzyme is most likely active in the

(1) nucleus                         (3) mitochondria
(2) vacuoles                        (4) chloroplasts

9. In several species of birds, the males show off their bright colors and long feathers. The dull colored females usually pick the brightest colored males for mates. Male offspring inherit their father's bright colors and long feathers. Compared to earlier generations, future generations of these birds will be expected to have a greater proportion of

(1) bright-colored females          (3) dull-colored males
(2) dull-colored females            (4) bright-colored males

10. Which human activity will most likely have a *negative* effect on global stability?

(1) decreasing water pollution levels
(2) increasing recycling programs
(3) decreasing habitat destruction
(4) increasing world population growth

11. Which statement describes starches, fats, proteins, and DNA?

(1) They are used to store genetic information.
(2) They are complex molecules made from smaller molecules.
(3) They are used to assemble larger inorganic materials.
(4) They are simple molecules used as energy sources.

12. *Salmonella* bacteria can cause humans to have stomach cramps, vomiting, diarrhea, and fever. The effect these bacteria have on humans indicates that *Salmonella* bacteria are

(1) predators

(2) pathogenic organisms

(3) parasitic fungi

(4) decomposers

13. Which order of metabolic processes converts nutrients consumed by an organism into cell parts?

(1) digestion — > absorption — > circulation — >diffusion — > synthesis

(2) absorption — > circulation — > digestion — > diffusion — >synthesis

(3) digestion — > synthesis — > diffusion — > circulation — > absorption

(4) synthesis — > absorption — > digestion — > diffusion — > circulation

*Base your answers to questions 14 and 15 on the information below and on your knowledge of biology.*

Lichens are composed of two organisms, a fungus that cannot make its own food and algae that contain chlorophyll. Lichens may live on the bark of trees or even on bare rock. They secrete acids that tend to break up the rock they live on, helping to produce soil. As soil accumulates from the broken rock and dead lichens, other organisms, such as plants, may begin to grow.

14. The ability of lichens to alter their environment, enabling other organisms to grow and take their places in that environment, is one step in the process of

(1) biological evolution

(2) ecological succession

(3) maintenance of cellular communication

(4) differentiation in complex organisms

15. What is the role of the algae component of a lichen in an ecosystem?

(1) decomposer

(2) parasite

(3) herbivore

(4) producer

**Day 19**

**Stop.** Check your answers and note how many correct **Points**

1. **2**      The key phrase in this question is "this discovery extended the ideas of inheritance that Gregor Mendel had discovered"

               This phrase indicates a modification of a previous scientific discovery.

2. **4**      Identical twins is a result of a single fertilized cell separating into two equal cells with the *same DNA.*

               Twins appearing different = Altered gene expression , likely, through *environmental factors.*

3. **2**      When genes are transferred from parents to offspring, the offspring *inherits* the characteristics of the parents.

4. **1**      Raw meat contains bacteria and other microbes that may be harmful to human.

               Cooking kills these bacteria and microbes.

5. **3**      Carbon dioxide, water, and oxygen (inorganic) and glucose (organic) are substances that are involve n in photosynthesis and cellular respiration processes.

6. **1**      The key phrase in this question is "certain bacteria are resistant."

               The fact that *only* certain ones are resistant means that antibiotics were effective in killing most of the bacteria.

**7. 2**      The key phrase in this question is "pass from fetus to mother"

Wastes ($CO_2$) = from fetus to mother through the placenta.

Nutrients (all the others) = from mother to fetus

**8. 4**      Carbon dioxide = needed for photosynthesis.

Chloroplast = photosynthesis organelle
The enzyme, rubisco, will be most active in the chloroplast.

**9. 4**      Based on the information provided in the question, Choice 4 conclusion is the most reasonable of all the choices given

**10. 4**      The key phrase in the question is *"negative effect"*

Of all the activities given as choices, increasing world population will likely have a negative effect on global stability because more natural resources will be used up, as well as more habitats being destroyed to accommodate the increase in the population.

All of the other activities will have positive effects on global stability.

**11. 2**      The molecules given are all complex molecules because each is composed of repeated units of smaller molecules.

Carbohydrates: composed of simple sugars (monosaccharides)

Fats      : composed of glycerides

Protein:      : composed of amino acids

DNA      : composed of base sequences

12. **2**    The symptoms (diarrhea, vomiting, fever..etc) caused by salmonella bacteria in human indicate that salmonella is a disease causing bacteria.

Pathogenic = disease causing.

13. **1**    *Digestion* (breakdown of food into nutrients) is the first metabolic process that occurs when food is eaten.

*Absorption* of the nutrients follows digestion.

14. **2**    The passage and question describe a process by which one organism replaces another in a changed environment.

This is a definition of ecological succession.

15. **4**    Since *algae* contain chlorophyll, they can carry out photosynthesis in the lichen ecosystem.

Only the *producers (algea)* can make their own energy through photosynthesis.

**Start:** Answer all questions on this day before stopping

1. The diagram below represents three human body systems.

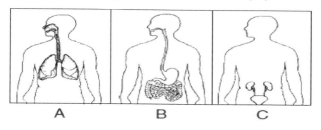

Which row in the chart below correctly shows what systems *A*, *B*, and *C* provide for the human body?

| Row | System A | System B | System C |
|-----|----------|----------|----------|
| (1) | blood cells | glucose | hormones |
| (2) | oxygen | absorption | gametes |
| (3) | gas exchange | nutrients | waste removal |
| (4) | immunity | coordination | carbon dioxide |

2. Which statement provides accurate information about the technique illustrated below?

Diseased African cotton plant

Healthy American cotton plant

Healthy cotton plant produced to grow in Africa

(1) This technique results in offspring that are genetically identical to the parents.

(2) New varieties of organisms can be developed by this technique known as selective breeding.

(3) This technique is used by farmers to eliminate mutations in future members of the species.

(4) Since the development of cloning, this technique is no longer used in agriculture.

3. The graph below shows the percent of variation for a given trait in four different populations of the same species. The populations inhabit similar environments.

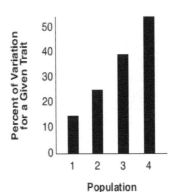

In which population will the greatest number of individuals most likely survive if a significant environmental change related to this trait occurs?

(1) 1                                       (3) 3
(2) 2                                         (4) 4

4. Which diagram best represents the relative locations of the structures in the list below?

A–chromosome
B–nucleus
C–cell
D–gene

    ( 1 )                ( 2 )                ( 3 )                ( 4 )

5. The diagram below represents two single-celled organisms.

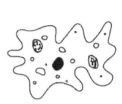 

These organisms carry out the activities needed to maintain homeostasis by using specialized internal

(1) tissues                              (3) systems
(2) organelles                           (4) organs

6. A researcher recently discovered a new species of bacteria in the body of a tubeworm living near a hydrothermal vent. He compared the DNA of this new bacterial species to the DNA of four other species of bacteria. The DNA sequences came from the same part of the bacterial chromosome of all four species.

| Species | DNA Sequence |
|---|---|
| unknown species | ACT GCA CCC |
| species I | ACA GCA CCG |
| species II | ACT GCT GGA |
| species III | ACA GCA GGG |
| species IV | ACT GCA CCG |

According to these data, the unknown bacterial species is most closely related to

(1) species I                            (3) species III
(2) species II                           (4) species IV

7. The diagram below represents a portion of a cell membrane.

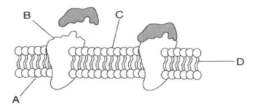

Which structure may function in the recognition of chemical signals?

(1) *A*                          (3) *C*
(2) *B*                          (4) *D*

8. Four students each drew an illustration to show the flow of energy in a field ecosystem. Which illustration is most accurate?

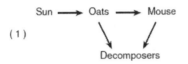

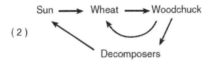

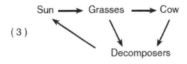

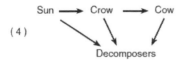

9. The diagram below represents an interaction between parts of an organism.

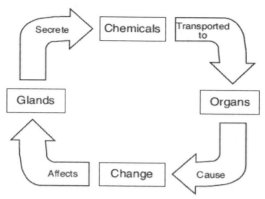

The term *chemicals* in this diagram represents

(1) starch molecules

(2) DNA molecules

(3) hormone molecules

(4) receptor molecules

10. A pattern of reproduction and growth in a one celled organism is shown below.

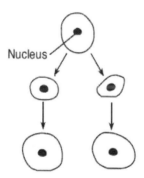

Which statement best describes this pattern of reproduction?

(1) All genetic material comes from one parent.

(2) Only some of the genetic material comes from one parent.

(3) The size of the parent determines the amount of genetic material.

(4) The size of the parent determines the source of the genetic material.

11. An experiment was carried out to determine which mouthwash was most effective against bacteria commonly found in the mouth. Four paper discs were each dipped into a different brand of mouthwash. The discs were then placed onto the surface of a culture plate that contained food, moisture, and bacteria commonly found in the mouth. The diagram below shows the growth of bacteria on the plate after 24 hours.

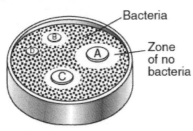

Which change in procedure would have improved the experiment?

(1) using a smaller plate with less food and moisture
(2) using bacteria from many habitats other than the mouth
(3) using the same size paper discs for each mouthwash
(4) using the same type of mouthwash on each disc

12. The evolutionary pathways of five species are represented in the diagram below.

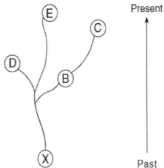

Which statement is supported by the diagram?

(1) Species *C* is the ancestor of species *B*.
(2) Species *D* and *E* evolved from species *B*.
(3) Species *X* evolved later than species *D* but before species *B*.
(4) Both species *C* and species *D* are related to species *X*.

---

13. The diagram below represents human reproductive systems.

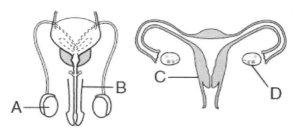

Which statement best describes part of the human reproductive process?

(1) Testosterone produced in *A* is transferred to *D*, where it influences embryonic development.

(2) Testosterone produced in *D* influences formation of sperm within *B*.

(3) Estrogen and progesterone influence the activity of *C*.

(4) Progesterone stimulates the division of the egg within *C*.

14. A sample of bacteria was added to a culture dish containing a food supply. The dish was kept in an incubator for two weeks, where temperature and other conditions that favored bacterial growth were kept constant. The graph below shows changes that occurred in the bacterial population over the two weeks.

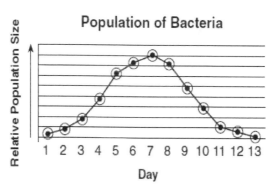

Which statement provides the best explanation for some of the changes observed?

(1) The bacteria were unable to reproduce until day 8.

(2) The bacteria consumed all of the available food.

(3) The culture dish contained an antibiotic for the first five days.

(4) The temperature increased and the bacteria died.

15. In an ecosystem, the herring population was reduced by fishermen. As a result, the tuna, which feed on the herring, disappeared. The sand eels, which are eaten by herring, increased in number. The fishermen then overharvested the sand eel population. Cod and seabirds then decreased. Which food web best represents the feeding relationships in this ecosystem?

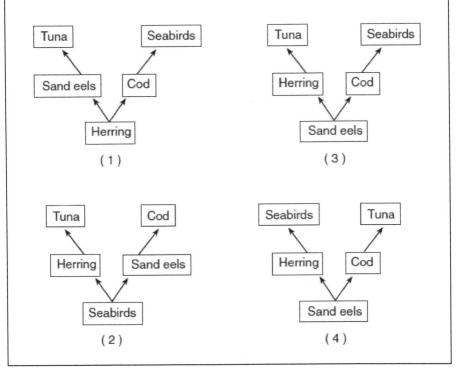

Day 20

**Stop.** Check your answers and note how many correct **Points**

1. **3**     Diagram A shows air way and lungs:
            System A is the respiratory system (gas exchange).

            Diagram B shows the stomach and intestine:
            System B is the digestive system (nutrient breakdown).

            Diagram C shows the kidney and bladder
            System C is the excretory system (waste removal).

2. **2**     Selective breeding is the process of combining traits from
            two or more varieties of organisms to produced an organism
            with desired characteristics.

3. **4**     A population with the greatest biodiversity (variation in traits)
            are the most likely to survive a significant environmental change.
            Population 4 has the greatest percent of variation.

4. **2**     This is a question of order of organization in which the least
            complex structure (A- gene) will be in the smallest inner
            circle, and the most complex (C-cell) will be in the outermost
            circle.

5. **2**     The organisms shown are amoeba and paramecium, which are
            single-celled organisms.

            These cell-organisms, just like human cells, contain organelles
            that carry out life functions.

6. **4**     The unknown species will be most closely related to the
            species with the most DNA sequence matches (Species IV)

7. **2**     The chemical is attached to B, therefore, B recognized the
            chemical signal.

**8. 1**     Energy flows from the sun to producers (oak plant) to consumers (mouse) to decomposers .

This energy flow is best illustrated in Choice 1.

Choice 3 is almost correct EXCEPT that energy is shown as being recycled back to the sun, which does not happen.

**9. 3**     Chemicals secreted by glands = *hormones.*

Hormones affect and regulate many life processes.

**10. 1**     Since the two identical cells come from the one-celled parent, their genetic materials also come from the one-celled parent.

**11. 3**     According to the diagram, different size paper discs (variable 1) were dipped in different brands of mouthwash (variable 2).

Accurate results cannot be collected about an experiment when there are two or more variables.

**12. 4**     According to the evolutionary tree, X is the common ancestor of all the other four species (B, C, D and E).

Choice 1: False. B is the ancestor C

Choice 2: False. D and E are related to B, *not evolved* from B.

Choice 3: False. X evolved earlier than all the other species.

*Choice 4: True. X is the common ancestor. All the species that come after X are related to X.*

13. **3**      Eliminate Choices 1 and 2 because hormones produced by males cannot be transferred to females (and vice versa) during reproductive processes.

Estrogen and progesterone are female hormones that regulate reproductive cycle, which includes the release of eggs from the ovary (D).

Choice 4 is incorrect because the main function of progesterone in reproduction is to stimulate the uterus lining to grow and be ready to carry the embryo as it develops.

14. **2**      According to the paragraph, everything was kept constant, except the food supply.

As the bacteria population grow, the food supply gets smaller. The sharp decrease in the bacteria population is likely due to the decrease in food supply.

15. **3**      According to the information in the question:

Sand eels are eaten by herring.

Herring are eaten by tuna.

Just from these relationships alone, the food web diagram in Choice 3 best illustrates these relations.

Start: Answer all questions on this day before stopping

*Base your answers to questions 1 and 2 on the information below and on your knowledge of biology.*

Two students each design their own investigations to determine whether resting or exercising beforehand allows a person to squeeze a clothespin more times over a certain period of time.

Student *A* squeezes the clothespin as many times as he can after sitting quietly for two minutes. In the second trial he runs in place for two minutes and then squeezes the clothespin as many times as he can. He records the results of each trial in his data table.

Student *B* uses the same procedure as student *A*. She also asks that the other 25 boys and girls in her class carry out the same procedure and she records their data. She then calculates the average number of times that the clothespins had been squeezed without exercise and with exercise before the trials.

1. Based on the description given of the investigations, state *one* reason why student *B*'s investigation will give more reliable results than student *A*'s. [1]

_____

_____


2. Student *B* states that exercising before the second trial will always have the same effect on this type of muscular activity. Explain why the statement made by student *B* could be questioned. [1]

_____

_____

*Base your answers to questions 3 and 4 on the information and table below and on your knowledge of biology.*

A model of a cell is prepared and placed in a beaker of fluid as shown in the diagram below. The letters *A*, *B*, and *C* represent substances in the initial experimental setup.

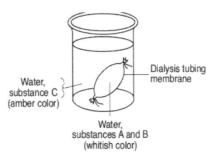

Water,
substance C
(amber color)

Dialysis tubing
membrane

Water,
substances A and B
(whitish color)

The table below summarizes the content and appearance of the cell model and beaker after 20 minutes.

**Results After 20 Minutes**

|  | Outside of Cell Model | Inside of Cell Model |
|---|---|---|
| Substances | water, A, C | water, A, B, C |
| Color | amber | blue black |

3. Complete the table below to summarize a change in location of substance *C* in the experimental setup. [3]

| Name of Substance C | Direction of Movement of Substance C | Reason for the Moveme of Substance C |
|---|---|---|
|  |  |  |

4. Identify substance *B* and explain why it did *not* move out of the model cell. [2]

Substance: _____

_____

_____

*Base your answers to questions 5 through 7 on the Universal Genetic Code Chart below and on your knowledge of biology.*

Some DNA, RNA, and amino acid information from the analysis of a gene present in five different species is shown in the chart on the next page.

## Universal Genetic Code Chart
### Messenger RNA Codons and Amino Acids for Which They Code

| | | Second base | | | | |
|---|---|---|---|---|---|---|
| | | U | C | A | G | |
| **First base** | **U** | UUU UUC } PHE / UUA UUG } LEU | UCU UCC UCA UCG } SER | UAU UAC } TYR / UAA UAG } STOP | UGU UGC } CYS / UGA } STOP / UGG } TRP | U C A G |
| | **C** | CUU CUC CUA CUG } LEU | CCU CCC CCA CCG } PRO | CAU CAC } HIS / CAA CAG } GLN | CGU CGC CGA CGG } ARG | U C A G |
| | **A** | AUU AUC AUA } ILE / AUG } MET or START | ACU ACC ACA ACG } THR | AAU AAC } ASN / AAA AAG } LYS | AGU AGC } SER / AGA AGG } ARG | U C A G |
| | **G** | GUU GUC GUA GUG } VAL | GCU GCC GCA GCG } ALA | GAU GAC } ASP / GAA GAG } GLU | GGU GGC GGA GGG } GLY | U C A G |

*(right side label: Third base)*

5. Using the Universal Genetic Code Chart, fill in the missing amino acids in the amino acid sequence for species *A* in the chart *below* [1]

6. Using the information given, fill in the missing mRNA bases in the mRNA strand for species *B* in the chart *below*. [1]

7. Using the information given, fill in the missing DNA bases in the DNA strand for species *C* in the chart *below* [1]

| Species A | DNA strand: | TAC | CGA | CCT | TCA |
| | mRNA strand: | AUG | GCU | GGA | AGU |
| | Amino acid sequence: | ____ | ____ | ____ | ____ |
| Species B | DNA strand: | TAC | TTT | GCA | GGA |
| | mRNA strand: | ____ | ____ | ____ | ____ |
| | Amino acid sequence: | MET | LYS | ARG | PRO |
| Species C | DNA strand: | ____ | ____ | ____ | ____ |
| | mRNA strand: | AUG | UUU | UGU | CCC |
| | Amino acid sequence: | MET | PHE | CYS | PRO |
| Species D | DNA strand: | TAC | GTA | GTT | GCA |
| | mRNA strand: | AUG | CAU | CAA | CGU |
| | Amino acid sequence: | MET | HIS | GLN | ARG |
| Species E | DNA strand: | TAC | TTC | GCG | GGT |
| | mRNA strand: | AUG | AAG | CGC | CCA |
| | Amino acid sequence | MET | LYS | ARG | PRO |

**Day 21**

**Stop.** Check your answers and note how many correct **Points**

# Day 21                          Answers and Explanations

**1. 1 point**   The bigger the sample size in an experiment, the more valid the results of the experiment.

**Acceptable responses include, but are not limited to:**

*Sample size is larger*

*Results are averaged*

*Including both males and females rather than just one sex*

**2. 1 point**   **Acceptable responses include, but are not limited to:**

*The students may not all be in similar physical condition.*

*Relatively small sample size used.*

*Not all people will respond in the same way.*

**3. 3 points**   Cell membranes are selectively permeable, so only molecules of certain sizes can pass across.

Your responses to questions 3 and 4 should reflect this fact.

**Acceptable responses include, but are not limited to:**

| Name of C (1 point) | Direction of movement of C (1 point) | Reason for movement of C (1 point) |
|---|---|---|
| *Starch* | *into model cell* | *small size of molecules* |
| *iodine* | *from high to low concentration* | *differences in concentration* |
| | | *diffusion* |

**4. 2 points**   **Acceptable 2-point responses include, but are not limited to:**

***Identifying substance B ( 1 point)***

*Starch*

*Polysaccharide*

*Complex carbohydrate*

***Explaining why B did not move out of the model cell (1 point)***

*It is a large molecule.*

*Too big*

5. 1 point      The only acceptable responses are:

                   *MET     ALA     GLY     SER*

                          **or**

                   *START    ALA     GLY     SER*


6. 1 point      The only acceptable response is:

                     *AUG    AAA    CGU     CCU*


7. 1 point      The only acceptable response is:

                     *TAC    AAA    ACA     GGG*

Start: Answer all questions on this day before stopping

1. An organelle that releases energy for metabolic activity in a nerve cell is the

   (1) chloroplast          (3) mitochondrion
   (2) ribosome             (4) vacuole

2. Estrogen has a direct effect on the

   (1) formation of a zygote
   (2) changes within the uterus
   (3) movement of an egg toward the sperm
   (4) development of a placenta within the ovary

3. Which procedure would most likely provide valid results in a test to determine if drug *A* would be effective in treating cancer in white mice?

   (1) injecting 1 mL of drug *A* into 100 white mice with cancer
   (2) injecting 1 mL of drug *A* into 100 white mice with cancer and 0.5 mL of drug *X* into 100 white mice without cancer
   (3) injecting 1 mL of drug *A* into 100 white mice with cancer and 0.5 mL of drug *X* into another group of 100 white mice with cancer
   (4) injecting 1 mL of drug *A* into 100 white mice with cancer and 1 mL of distilled water into another group of 100 white mice with cancer

4 Humans require organ systems to carry out life processes. Single-celled organisms do not have organ systems and yet they are able to carry out life processes. This is because

   (1) human organ systems lack the organelles found in single-celled organisms
   (2) a human cell is more efficient than the cell of a single-celled organism
   (3) it is not necessary for single-celled organisms to maintain homeostasis
   (4) organelles present in single-celled organisms act in a manner similar to organ systems

5. The sorting and recombining of genes during meiosis and fertilization usually leads to the production of

   (1) gametes with many copies of the same chromosome
   (2) embryos with traits identical to those of all other members of the species
   (3) zygotes with the genetic information to produce only females
   (4) offspring with some traits that did not appear in their parents

6. As women age, their reproductive cycles stop due to decreased

(1) digestive enzyme production
(2) production of ATP
(3) levels of specific hormones
(4) heart rate

7. Which statement about embryonic organ development in humans is accurate?

(1) It is affected primarily by the eating habits and general health of the father.
(2) It may be affected by the diet and general health of the mother.
(3) It will not be affected by any medication taken by the mother in the second month of pregnancy.
(4) It is not affected by conditions outside the embryo.

8. Which process illustrates a feedback mechanism in plants?

(1) Chloroplasts take in more nitrogen, which increases the rate of photosynthesis.
(2) Chloroplasts release more oxygen in response to a decreased rate of photosynthesis.
(3) Guard cells change the size of leaf openings, regulating the exchange of gases.
(4) Guard cells release oxygen from the leaf at night.

9. If several species of carnivores are removed from an ecosystem, the most likely effect on the ecosystem will be

(1) an increase in the kinds of autotrophs
(2) a decrease in the number of abiotic factors
(3) a decrease in stability among populations
(4) an increase in the rate of succession

10. Two proteins in the same cell perform different functions. This is because the two proteins are composed of

(1) chains folded the same way and the same sequence of simple sugars
(2) chains folded the same way and the same sequence of amino acids
(3) chains folded differently and a different sequence of simple sugars
(4) chains folded differently and a different sequence of amino acids

11. As succession proceeds from a shrub community to a forest community, the shrub community modifies its environment, eventually making it

(1) more favorable for itself and less favorable for the forest community
(2) more favorable for itself and more favorable for the forest community
(3) less favorable for itself and more favorable for the forest community
(4) less favorable for itself and less favorable for the forest community

12. Which sequence represents the order of some events in human development?

(1) zygote → sperm → tissues → egg
(2) fetus → tissues → zygote → egg
(3) zygote → tissues → organs → fetus
(4) sperm → zygote → organs → tissues

13. Scientists have genetically altered a common virus so that it can destroy the most lethal type of brain tumor without harming the healthy tissue nearby. This technology is used for all of the following *except*

(1) treating the disease
(2) curing the disease
(3) controlling the disease
(4) diagnosing the disease

14. In state forests and parks containing varieties of flowering trees and shrubs, there are signs that say "Take nothing but pictures, leave nothing but footprints." These signs are necessary because

(1) humans can destroy habitats by removing flowering trees and shrubs
(2) all animals feed directly on flowering shrubs that may be removed by people
(3) removal of flowering trees and shrubs will increase biodiversity
(4) flowering shrubs grow best in state forests and parks

15. Which statement best describes the flow of energy and the movement of chemical compounds in an ecosystem?

(1) Energy flows into living organisms and remains there, while chemical compounds are transferred from organism to organism.
(2) Chemical compounds flow in one direction in a food chain and energy is produced.
(3) Energy is transferred from organism to organism in a food chain and chemical compounds are recycled.
(4) Energy flows out of living organisms and is lost, while chemical compounds remain permanently inside organisms.

**Day 22**

**Stop.** Check your answers and note how many correct **Points**

# Track Your Progress

If you have completed days 13, 16, 19 and 22 multiple choice question sets, you can easily check your progress and improvements in this question category.
. Go to page 273

. Plot and graph the number of points you got correct on each of the days using the first graph on the page (the 15-point graph).

You hope to see an upward trend on the graph, which indicates improvement and progress.

If you are not satisfied with your performance and progress, it is highly recommended that you study a bit more from your review packets and books before continuing on to the next sets of questions in this book.

1. **3**        Energy is produced during cellular respiration, which occurs in the mitochondria.

2. **2**        Estrogen = reproductive hormone = affects the uterus.

3. **4**        When testing to see the effect of a drug on a disease, equal amounts (1 mL) of the drug (drug A) and placebo (distilled water) must be given to two groups with equal numbers of individual (100 white mice) with the same disease (cancer).

Experiment group = receive drug A

Control group = receiving distilled water (placebo)

Data (in this case the number of cancer cells or the size of tumor) from the two groups can be collected and compared. Any difference in data is due to the effect of the drug.

The result will be considered valid since all other factors were the same for both groups.

4. **4**        All life functions performed by each organ system are carried out within the organelles of the cells.

A single-celled organism also contains organelles that carry out life processes in the same manners as the cell organelles found in organ systems of humans.

The only difference is that these life processes are more complex in human cells than in single-celled organisms.

5. **4**        The key phrase in this question is "sorting and recombining genes"

sorting and recombining genes = mixing of genes of parents

Mixed genes = mixed traits unlike those of the parents

6. **3**       Women reproductive cycles (also known as menstrual cycles) are control by estrogen and progesterone (which are hormones).

           Changes in hormone levels = Changes in reproductive cycles

7. **1**       Eliminate Choice 1 because embryonic development occurs within the uterus of the mother (not father).

           Since embryonic development occurs within the uterus of the mother, and there is a connection through the placenta between the mother and embryo, the health and diet of the mother will certainly affect how the embryo develops.

8. **3**       Feedback mechanism = adjusts and *regulates* activities to maintain homeostasis.

9. **3**       Removing several species of one organism from an ecosystem will disturb the balance (stability) of the population .

10. **4**       Proteins = composed of amino acids. (Eliminate Choices 1 and 3)

           Of the two choices remaining, Choice 4 best describes why the different proteins perform different function.

11. **3**       The process described in the question is ecological succession.

           Ecological succession = when a change in environment brings changes in species structure of a community.

           Ecological succession only occurs when the changes in the environment are *less favorable to the species* that were already there (*shrub community*) and *more favorable* to the new species (*forest community*).

**12. 3**       In a human development:

*Zygote* forms form the fertilization of egg by sperm

*Tissues* form from mitosis and differentiation of the zygote

*Organs* form from organization of tissues

*Fetus* develops from organs working together.

**13. 4**       The key phrase in this question is "destroy the most lethal type of tumor"

Destroying tumor = treating, curing, or controlling cancer.

Eliminate Choices A, B and C.

Diagnosing a disease (Choice D) does not involve destroying the disease causing agent.

**14. 1**       Taking anything (other than picture) from a habitat may cause a series of negative effects that can destabilize and destroy the habitat.

**15. 3**       *For an ecosystem to survive:*

Energy must be *transferred* from producers to consumers to decomposers.

Chemical compounds released as wastes by one organism (or from decomposed organisms) are used by others (*recycled*) to perform crucial life functions that will keep the energy cycle going.

Start: Answer all questions on this day before stopping

1. Which row in the chart below contains correct information concerning synthesis?

| Row | Building Blocks | Substance Synthesized Using the Building Blocks |
|-----|-----------------|-------------------------------------------------|
| (1) | glucose molecules | DNA |
| (2) | simple sugars | protein |
| (3) | amino acids | enzyme |
| (4) | molecular bases | starch |

2. Which statement about the gametes represented in the diagram below is correct?

(1) They are produced by females.
(2) They are fertilized in an ovary.
(3) They transport genetic material.
(4) They are produced by mitosis.

3. The diagram below illustrates asexual reproduction in yeast.

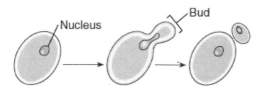

Yeast produce offspring that usually have

(1) genes that are different from those of the parent
(2) genes that are identical to those of the parent
(3) half of the genetic information of the parent
(4) organelles that are not found in the parent

4. Some interactions in a desert community are shown in the diagram below.

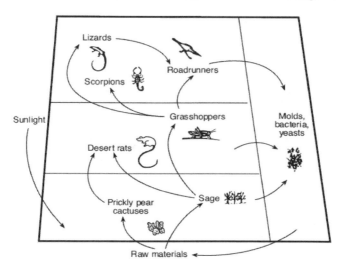

Which statement is a valid inference based on the diagram?

(1) Certain organisms may compete for vital resources.
(2) All these organisms rely on energy from decomposers.
(3) Organisms synthesize energy.
(4) All organisms occupy the same niche.

5. The growth of a population is shown in the graph below.

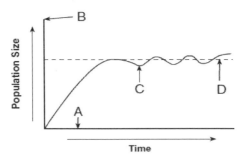

Which letter indicates the carrying capacity of the environment for this population?

(1) *A*                              (3) *C*
(2) *B*                              (4) *D*

6. The diagram below illustrates some functions of the pituitary gland. The pituitary gland secretes substances that, in turn, cause other glands to secrete different substances.

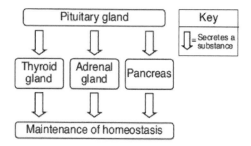

Which statement best describes events shown in the diagram?

(1) Secretions provide the energy needed for metabolism.

(2) The raw materials for the synthesis of secretions come from nitrogen.

(3) The secretions of all glands speed blood circulation in the body.

(4) Secretions help the body to respond to changes from the normal state

7. The diagram below represents a section of a molecule that carries genetic information.

The pattern of numbers represents

(1) a sequence of paired bases

(2) the order of proteins in a gene

(3) folds of an amino acid

(4) positions of gene mutations

8. The diagram below illustrates some of the changes that occur during gamete formation.

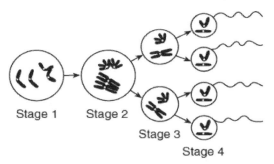

Which graph best represents the changes in the amount of DNA in one of the cells at each stage?

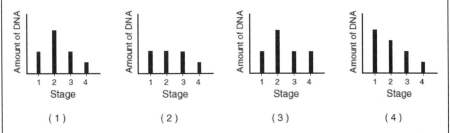

9. Which life functions are directly regulated through feedback mechanisms associated with the actions of the structures labeled *X*?

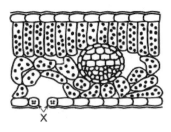

(1) excretion and immunity
(2) digestion and coordination
(3) circulation and reproduction
(4) respiration and photosynthesis

10. Which concept is best represented in the diagram shown below?

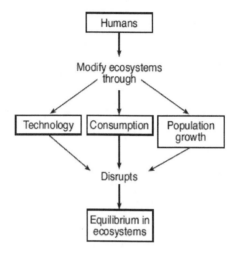

(1) Human actions are a threat to equilibrium in ecosystems.
(2) Equilibrium in ecosystems requires that humans modify ecosystems.
(3) Equilibrium in ecosystems directly affects how humans modify ecosystems.
(4) Human population growth is the primary reason for equilibrium in ecosystems.

11. Which evolutionary tree best represents the information in the chart?

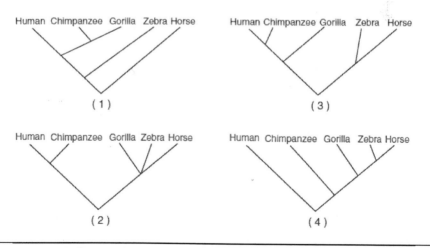

12. A food chain is illustrated below.

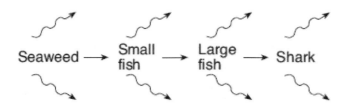

Seaweed → Small fish → Large fish → Shark

The arrows represented as ⌇⌇⌇➤ most likely indicate

(1) energy released into the environment as heat
(2) oxygen produced by respiration
(3) the absorption of energy that has been synthesized
(4) the transport of glucose away from the organism

13. Which set of terms best identifies the letters in the diagram below?

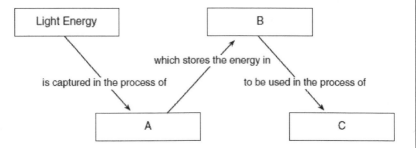

|     | A              | B                   | C             |
|-----|----------------|---------------------|---------------|
| (1) | photosynthesis | inorganic molecules | decomposition |
| (2) | respiration    | organic molecules   | digestion     |
| (3) | photosynthesis | organic molecules   | respiration   |
| (4) | respiration    | inorganic molecules | photosynthesis |

14. Within which structure shown in the diagram below are energy-rich organic compounds used to produce ATP?

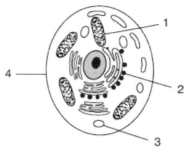

(1) 1                          (3) 3
(2) 2                          (4) 4

15. The diagram below shows the relative concentration of molecules inside and outside of a cell.

 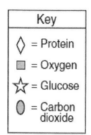

| Key | |
|---|---|
| ◇ | = Protein |
| ▫ | = Oxygen |
| ☆ | = Glucose |
| ◖ | = Carbon dioxide |

Which statement best describes the general direction of diffusion across the membrane of this cell?

(1) Glucose would diffuse into the cell.
(2) Protein would diffuse out of the cell.
(3) Carbon dioxide would diffuse out of the cell.
(4) Oxygen would diffuse into the cell.

**Day 23**

**Stop.** Check your answers and note how many correct **Points**

1. **3**  Amino acids = building blocks for proteins.

Enzymes are proteins.

2. **3**  All gametes (sperm or egg) carry genetic information.

3. **2**  Asexual reproduction = offsprings identical to parents

4. **1**  One important information from the food web is that two or more organisms in the community do eat the same food .

Two or more organisms eating the same food = *Competition*

5. **4**  *Carrying capacity* = maximum population size of a species that the environment can sustain.

Population usually fluctuates slightly above and below the carrying capacity (D).

6. **4**  The key information provided by the diagram is that chemical substances secreted by the glands and pancreas are involved in maintaining homeostasis.

The body maintains homeostasis by responding and adjusting to changes from the normal level of secretions.

7. **1**  The diagram shown is of a chromosome (double helix).

Chromosomes are composed of base-pair sequences, which are represented by the numbers on the diagram.

**8. 1**    Just by looking at one cell at each stage, you can see that a Stage 2 cell has the most number of DNA strands and a Stage 4 cell has the least number of DNA strands.

for Choice 1 graph best shows these strand comparisons.

**9. 4**    Structures X in the leaf cross-section are the guard cells.

Guard cells  = regulate movements of $H_2O$ and $CO_2$

These two substances are involved in respiration and photosynthesis.

**10. 1**    "Modification" of any kind to an ecosystem is a threat (Choice 1) to the ecosystem.

**11. 3**    *Based on knowledge and experience:*
Horses and zebras are close relatives; so they will branch off the same ancestor.

Humans, chimpanzees, and gorillas are close relatives; so they will branch off the same ancestor.
Choice 3 graph best shows these evolutionary relationships.

**12. 1**    The purpose of a food chain diagram is to show the *energy transfer* from one level of organisms to another. Eliminate Choices 2 and 4 because these choices do not include energy.

⟶     represents energy transfer between the organisms.

〰⟶     represents heat energy that is released by the organisms since not every available energy at one level is transferred to the next level.

13. **3**  A is a process that uses light energy ( photosynthesis)

B is a product of photosynthesis (sugar; an organic molecule)

C is a process that uses sugar (cellular respiration)

14. **1**  ATP = product of cellular respiration = in mitochondria (1).

15. **3**  Diffusion of a substance across a cell membrane is from the side of high concentration to the side of low concentration.

Based on the diagram, there are more carbon dioxide inside than outside the cell. So carbon dioxide will diffuse out of the cell.

Substances in each of the other choice will not diffuse as stated because movements will be from low to high.

# Track Your Progress

If you have completed days 14, 17, 20 and 23 multiple choice question sets with graphs, tables, and diagrams, you can easily check your progress and improvements in this question category.
. Go to page 274

. Plot and graph the number of points you got correct on each of the days using the first graph on the page (the 15-point graph).

You hope to see an upward trend on the graph, which indicates improvement and progress.

If you are not satisfied with your performance and progress, it is highly recommended that you study a bit more from your review packets and books before continuing on to the next sets of questions in this book.

Start: Answer all questions on this day before stopping

---

*Base your answers to questions 1 through 3 on the information below and on your knowledge of biology.*

Human reproduction is influenced by many different factors.

1. Identify *one* reproductive hormone and state the role it plays in reproduction. [1]

_____

_____

2. Identify the structure in the uterus where the exchange of material between the mother and the developing fetus takes place. [1]

_____

3. Identify *one* harmful substance that can pass through this structure and describe the *negative* effect it can have on the fetus. [1]

_____

_____

---

*Base your answers to questions 4. and 5 on the information and data table below and on your knowledge of biology*

Two students collected data on their pulse rates while performing different activities. Their average results are shown in the data table below.

**Data Table**

| Activity | Average Pulse Rate (beats/min) |
|---|---|
| sitting quietly | 70 |
| walking | 98 |
| running | 120 |

4. State the relationship between activity and pulse rate. [1]

_____

5. State *one* way that this investigation could be improved. [1]

_____

_____

*Base your answers to questions 6 and 7 on the information below and on your knowledge of biology.*

A student read a magazine article that claimed people who exercise for 30 minutes are able to solve more math problems than if they had not exercised. The student convinced four of his friends to test this claim. First, he gave them 15 minutes to do 50 math problems. The number each person solved is shown in the trial 1 graph. Next, all four of the students exercised for 30 minutes. At the end of the 30 minutes, they were given another 50 math problems of equal difficulty for the same amount of time. The number of math problems each student solved is shown in the trial 2 graph.

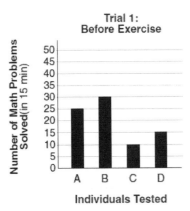
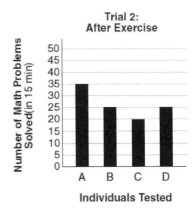

6. Explain why exercise could influence the ability of a student to solve math problems. [1]

_____

_____

7. State whether or not exercising for 30 minutes improved the ability of students to solve math problems. Support your answer using data from the graphs. [1]

_____

_____

*Base your answers to questions 8 through 10 on the diagram of a microscope below and on your knowledge of biology.*

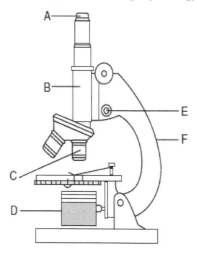

8. Information about which *two* lettered parts is needed in order to determine the total magnification of an object viewed with the microscope in the position shown? [1]

_____ and _____

9. Which lettered part should be used to focus the image while using high power? [1]

_____

10. State *two* ways the image seen through the microscope differs from the actual specimen being observed. [1]

_____ and _____

**Day 24**

**Stop.** Check your answers and note how many correct **Points**

1. **1 point:**  **Acceptable responses include, but are not limited to:**

   *Testosterone influences the formation of sperm cells.*

   *Testosterone influences the formation of gametes.*

   *Estrogen regulates female reproductive cycles*

   *Estrogen builds up the uterine lining for implantation and development of the embryo.*

   *Progesterone maintains uterine lining during pregnancy*

2. **1 point**  **Only the response below is acceptable:**

   *Placenta*

3. **1 point**  **Acceptable responses include, but are not limited to:**

   *drugs    – fetal addiction*

   *alcohol – low birth weight or premature birth or brain damage or fetal alcohol syndrome*

   *nicotine – brain damage or low birth weight*

   *Viruses, such as HIV, can cross the placenta putting the fetus at risk of disease or defects.*

4. **1 point**  **Acceptable responses include, but are not limited to:**

   *As activity increases, so does the pulse rate.*

   *The pulse rate increases as the activity increases.*

5. **1 point**  **Acceptable responses include, but are not limited to:**

   *Larger sample size*

   *Repeat the investigation*

**6. 1 point**      **Acceptable responses include, but are not limited to:**

*The blood will bring more oxygen to the brain.*

*Increased blood flow will remove wastes from the brain.*

*Increased blood flow brings more glucose (food molecules) to the brain.*

**7. 1 point**      *Note:* Your answer could be a "yes" or "no". However, your answer must be correctly explained for the point to be earned.

**Acceptable responses include, but are not limited to:**

*Yes, because three of the four students solved more problems after exercise.*

*No, because one student did fewer problems.*

*Cannot tell because there are only results from four students*

*Cannot tell because there are no data for a separate control group*

**8. 1 point**      **Only the response below is acceptable:**

*Both A and C.*

**9. 1 point**      **Only the response below is acceptable:**

*E.*

**10. 1 point**      **Two responses must be stated.**

**Acceptable responses include, but are not limited to:**

*Enlarged*

*Upside down*

*Backward*

*More detail*

---

# Track Your Progress

If you have completed days 15, 18, 21 and 24 short answer question sets, you can easily check your progress and improvements in this question category.

. Go to page 274

. Plot and graph the number of points you got correct on each of the days using the first graph on the page (the 10-point graph).

You hope to see an upward trend on the graph, which indicates improvement and progress.

If you are not satisfied with your performance and progress, it is highly recommended that you study a bit more from your review packets and books before continuing on to the next sets of questions in this book.

Start: Answer all questions on this day before stopping

1. The sickle-cell trait is an inherited condition resulting from the presence of abnormal molecules of the protein hemoglobin in red blood cells. A person with the sickle-cell trait may have a child with the same condition because the child receives from the parent

    (1) abnormal red blood cells
    (2) abnormal hemoglobin molecules
    (3) a code for the production of abnormal hemoglobin
    (4) a code for the production of abnormal amino acids

2. The diagram below represents the bones of the forelimbs of two animals alive today that most likely evolved from a common ancestor. Members of the original ancestral population were isolated into two groups by natural events.

    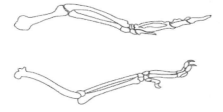

    If these two animals did have a common ancestor, which statement would best explain why there are differences in the bones?

    (1) Changes occurred to help the animals return to their original environment.
    (2) Changes contributed to the survival of the organisms in their new environment.
    (3) Changes helped reduce competition within each group.
    (4) Changes indicate the species are evolving to be more like the ancestral species.

3. When a planarian (a type of worm) is cut in half, each half usually grows back into a complete worm over time. This situation most closely resembles

    (1) asexual reproduction in which a mutation has occurred
    (2) sexual reproduction in which each half represents one parent
    (3) asexual reproduction of a single-celled organism
    (4) sexual reproduction of a single-celled organism

4. Damage to which structure will most directly disrupt water balance within a single-celled organism?

(1) ribosome                                  (3) nucleus
(2) cell membrane                             (4) chloroplast

5. Which sequence best represents the relationship between DNA and the traits of an organism?

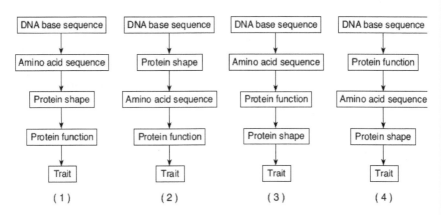

6. The diagram below represents the genetic contents of cells before and after a specific reproductive process.

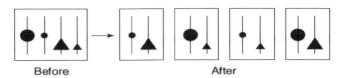

This process is considered a mechanism of evolution because it

(1) decreases the chance for new combinations of inheritable traits in a species
(2) decreases the probability that genes can be passed on to other body cells
(3) increases the chance for variations in offspring
(4) increases the number of offspring an organism can produce

7. Ecosystems will have a greater chance of maintaining equilibrium over a long period of time if they have

(1) organisms imported by humans from other environments
(2) a sudden change in climate
(3) a diversity of organisms
(4) predators eliminated from the food chains

*Base your answers to questions 8 through 11 on the diagram below and on your knowledge of biology.*

The diagram represents a single-celled organism, such as an ameba, undergoing the changes shown.

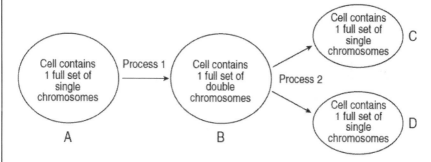

8. As a result of these processes, the single-celled organism accomplishes

(1) gamete production
(2) energy production
(3) sexual reproduction
(4) asexual reproduction

9. Process 1 is known as

(1) replication
(2) meiosis
(3) differentiation
(4) digestion

10. Process 1 and process 2 are directly involved in

(1) meiotic cell division
(2) mitotic cell division
(3) fertilization
(4) recombination

11. The genetic content of *C* is usually identical to the genetic content of

(1) *B* but not *D*
(2) both *B* and *D*
(3) *D* but not *A*
(4) both *A* and *D*

12. The diagram below represents the distribution of some molecules inside and outside of a cell over time.

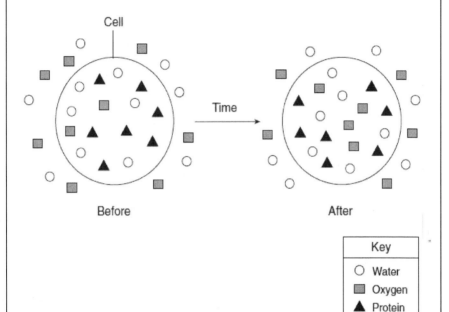

Before        Time        After

| Key | |
|---|---|
| ○ | Water |
| ▢ | Oxygen |
| ▲ | Protein |

Which factor prevented the protein molecules (▲) from moving out of the cell?

(1) temperature
(2) pH
(3) molecule size
(4) molecule concentration

*Base your answers to questions 13 through 15 on the information below and on your knowledge of biology.*

Honeybees have a very cooperative way of living. Scout bees find food, return to the hive, and do the "waggle dance" to communicate the location of the food source to other bees in the hive. The waggle, represented by the wavy line in the diagram below, indicates the direction of the food source, while the speed of the dance indicates the distance to the food. Different species of honeybees use the same basic dance pattern in slightly different ways as shown in the table below.

| Number of Waggle Runs in 15 Seconds | | Distance to Food (feet) |
|---|---|---|
| Giant Honeybee | Indian Honeybee | |
| 10.6 | 10.5 | 50 |
| 9.6 | 8.3 | 200 |
| 6.7 | 4.4 | 1000 |
| 4.8 | 2.8 | 2000 |

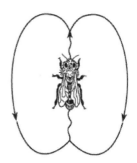

13. State the relationship between the distance to the food source and the number of waggle runs in 15 seconds. [1]

_____

_____

14. Explain how waggle-dance behavior increases the reproductive success of the bees. [1]

_____

_____

15. The number of waggle runs in 15 seconds for each of these species is most likely due to

(1) behavioral adaptation as a result of natural selection
(2) replacement of one species by another as a result of succession
(3) alterations in gene structure as a result of diet
(4) learned behaviors inherited as a result of asexual reproduction

*Base your answers to questions 16 through 20 on the information below and on your knowledge of biology.*

In a test for diabetes, blood samples were taken from an individual every 4 hours for 24 hours. The glucose concentrations were recorded and are shown in the data table below.

### Blood Glucose Level Over Time

| Time (h) | Blood Glucose Concentration (mg/dL) |
|----------|-------------------------------------|
| 0 | 100 |
| 4 | 110 |
| 8 | 128 |
| 12 | 82 |
| 16 | 92 |
| 20 | 130 |
| 24 | 104 |

16. State *one* likely cause of the change in blood glucose concentration between hour 16 and hour 20. [1]

_____

_____

*Directions (17 and 18): Using the information given, construct a line graph on the grid on the next page, following the directions below.*

17. Mark an appropriate scale on the axis labeled "Blood Glucose Concentration (mg/dL)." [1]

18. Plot the data from the data table. Surround each point with a small circle and connect the points. [1]

Example:

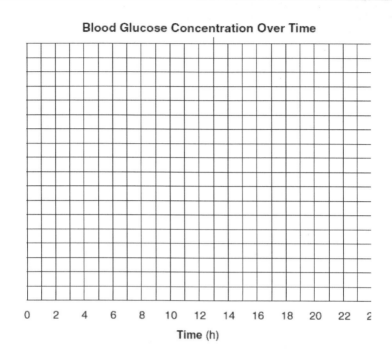

**Blood Glucose Concentration Over Time**

19. How might these results be different if this individual was *not* able to produce sufficient levels of insulin?

(1) The level of blood glucose would be constant.
(2) The average level of blood glucose would be lower.
(3) The maximum level of blood glucose would be higher.
(4) The minimum level of blood glucose would be lower.

20. The chemical that is responsible for the *decrease* in blood glucose concentration is released by

(1) muscle cells                    (3) the ovaries
(2) guard cells                     (4) the pancreas

**Day 25**

**Stop.** Check your answers and note how many correct **Points**

1. **3**  Inherit = receiving genetic codes for the abnormal hemoglobin

2. **2**  Based on the diagrams, there are obvious differences in the bone structures of the two forelimbs.

   Two related species of animals grow slightly different structures for the same body part so each can adapt better to their environment.

   Adaptation = changing traits to survive a changed environment.

3. **3**  In order for each half of the worm to grow back into a complete worm (as stated in the question), each half must have a way of making genetically identical cells of the half that was lost.

   Producing identical copies = asexually reproduction, which is common among single-cell organisms.

4. **2**  Water enters and exits a cell through the cell membrane.

5. **1**  Eliminate Choices 2 and 4 because amino acids codes for protein. These choices have it the other way around.

   Of the remaining choices, Choice 1 is best because proteins are shaped to perform specific functions, NOT the other way as illustrated in Choice 3

6. **3**  The cells AFTER the reproductive process contain different combinations of the genetic materials found in the cell BEFORE the reproductive process.
   *Different combinations of genetic materials* = increase variation of offsprings.

   Producing offsprings with varying characteristics that can help them *evolve* and survive in a changing environment.

7. **3**      Equilibrium in an ecosystem means that the needs of all organisms are met, and the conditions of the ecosystem are stable for a long period of time.

Eliminate Choices 1, 2 and 4. These conditions will destabilize any ecosystem.

Choice 3 is correct because biodiversity ensures that there will be varieties of organisms to perform different vital roles, and the needs of all organisms will be met in that ecosystem.

8. **4**      The diagrams illustrate a single-celled organism (A) producing two identical offspring cells ( C and D).

This is a characteristic of asexual reproduction.

9. **1**      The difference between cell A and B is that the number of chromosomes of B is doubled that of A.

Process 1, therefore, replicates chromosomes of A.

10. **2**      Asexual reproduction = mitosis (mitotic cell division).

11. **4**      Since this is an asexual reproduction (as stated above), offsprings C and D have identical genetic contents as those of parent A.

12. **3**      Eliminate Choices 1 and 2 because no information in this question is given about temperature and pH.

Eliminate Choice 4 because the concentration of protein is greater inside than outside, the protein should be able to pass from inside to outside through the cell membrane.

Choice 3 is correct because cell membranes have selective permeability, and can only let molecules of certain sizes pass through.

    

13. **1 point**  Acceptable responses include, but are not limited to:

*The closer the food source, the more waggle runs in 15 seconds.*

*Fewer waggles mean that food is farther away.*

*As one variable increases, the other decreases.*

14. **1 point**  Acceptable responses include, but are not limited to:

*If bees have better access to food, they can produce more offspring.*

*Finding food is easier, thus more bees can exist.*

15. **1**  Since the waggle dance is a way of communicating to help other bees find food, it is a good behavioral adaptation because it will help ensure the survival of the species.

16. **1 point**  Acceptable responses include, but are not limited to:

*The individual ate.*

*Insulin level dropped*

17. **1 point**  For marking appropriate scale on the axis.

18. **1 point**  For correctly plotting the data and connecting the points.

See example 2-points response for questions 17 and 18 on the next page.

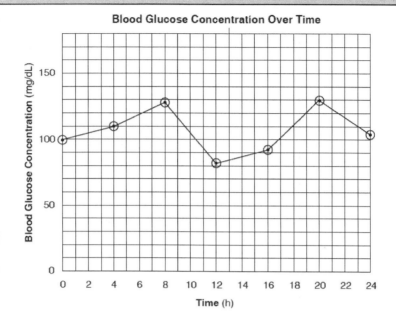

Blood Glucose Concentration Over Time

Allow credit if the points are correctly plotted but *not* circled.

Do *not* allow credit for plotting points that are not in the data table, e.g., (0,0), or for extending lines beyond the data points.

19. **3**     Insulin is a hormone produce in the islets of Langerhans in the pancreas to regulate blood sugar level.

Insufficient insulin levels production leads to high blood glucose (sugar) level, and the development of diabetes.

20. **4**     *See the above explanation.*

---

Start: Answer all questions on this day before stopping

1. The largest amount of DNA in a plant cell is contained in
   (1) a nucleus
   (2) a chromosome
   (3) a protein molecule
   (4) an enzyme molecule

2. Competition between two species occurs when
   (1) mold grows on a tree that has fallen in the forest
   (2) chipmunks and squirrels eat sunflower seeds in a garden
   (3) a crow feeds on the remains of a rabbit killed on the road
   (4) a lion stalks, kills, and eats an antelope

*Base your answers to questions 3 through 5 on the diagram below that shows some evolutionary pathways. Each letter represents a different species.*

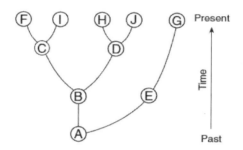

3. Which two organisms are most closely related?
   (1) *F* and *I*                    (3) *A* and *G*
   (2) *F* and *H*                    (4) *G* and *J*

4. The most recent ancestor of organisms *D* and *F* is
   (1) *A*                            (3) *C*
   (2) *B*                            (4) *I*

5. If *A* represents a simple multicellular heterotrophic organism, *B* would most likely represent
   (1) a single-celled photosynthetic organism
   (2) an autotrophic mammal
   (3) a complex multicellular virus
   (4) another type of simple multicellular heterotroph

6. The diagram below represents events associated with a biochemical process that occurs in some organisms.

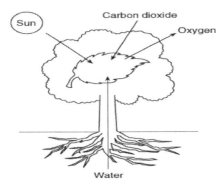

Which statement concerning this process is correct?

(1) The process represented is respiration and the primary source of energy for the process is the Sun.

(2) The process represented is photosynthesis and the primary source of energy for the process is the Sun.

(3) This process converts energy in organic compounds into solar energy which is released into the atmosphere.

(4) This process uses solar energy to convert oxygen into carbon dioxide.

7. The graph below shows the relative concentrations of certain hormones in the blood during the human female reproductive cycle.

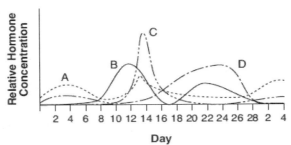

Which hormone has the lowest concentration on which day?

(1) hormone *A* on day 4                (3) hormone *C* on day 12

(2) hormone *B* on day 2                (4) hormone *D* on day 20

8. Four environmental factors are listed below.

> *A.* energy
> *B.* water
> *C.* oxygen
> *D.* minerals

Which factors limit environmental carrying capacity in a land ecosystem?

(1) *A,* only                                  (3) *A, C,* and *D,* only

(2) *B, C,* and *D,* only                  (4) *A, B, C,* and *D*

***Base your answers to questions 9 through 12 on the information below and on
your knowledge of biology.***

> Carbon, like many other elements, is maintained in ecosystems through
> a natural cycle. Human activities have been disrupting the carbon cycle.

9. Identify *one* process involved in recycling carbon dioxide within ecosystems. [1]

_____

10. State *one* reason why the amount of carbon dioxide in the atmosphere has
increased in the last 100 years. [1]

_____

_____

11. Identify *one* effect this increase in carbon dioxide could have on the
environment.[1]

_____

_____

12. Describe *one* way individuals can help slow down or reverse the increase in
carbon dioxide. [1]

_____

_____

*Base your answers to questions 13 through 16 on the information below and on your knowledge of biology.*

To demonstrate techniques used in DNA analysis, a student was given two paper strip samples of DNA. The two DNA samples are shown below.

**Sample 1:** ATTCCGGTAATCCCGTAATGCCGGATAATACTCCGGTAATATC

**Sample 2:** ATTCCGGTAATCCCGTAATGCCGGATAATACTCCGGTAATATC

The student cut between the C and G in each of the shaded CCGG sequences in sample 1 and between the As in each of the shaded TAAT sequences in sample 2. Both sets of fragments were then arranged on a paper model of a gel.

13. The action of what kind of molecules was being demonstrated when the DNA samples were cut? [1]

_____

14. Identify the technique that was being demonstrated when the fragments were arranged on the gel model. [1]

_____

15. The results of this type of DNA analysis are often used to help determine

(1) the number of DNA molecules in an organism
(2) if two species are closely related
(3) the number of mRNA molecules in DNA
(4) if two organisms contain carbohydrate molecules

16. State *one* way that the arrangement of the two samples on the gel model would differ. [1]

_____

_____

*Base your answers to questions 17 through 20 on the passage below and on your knowledge of biology.*

### Avian (Bird) Flu

Avian flu virus H5N1 has been a major concern recently. Most humans have not been exposed to this strain of the virus, so they have not produced the necessary protective substances. A vaccine has been developed and is being made in large quantities. However, much more time is needed to manufacture enough vaccine to protect most of the human population of the world.

Most flu virus strains affect the upper respiratory tract, resulting in a runny nose and sore throat. However, the H5N1 virus seems to go deeper into the lungs and causes severe pneumonia, which may be fatal for people infected by this virus.

So far, this virus has not been known to spread directly from one human to another. As long as H5N1 does not change to another strain that can be transferred from one human to another, a worldwide epidemic of the virus probably will not occur.

17. State *one* difference between the effect on the human body of the usual forms of flu virus and the effect of H5N1. [1]

_____

_____

18. Identify the type of substance produced by the human body that protects against antigens, such as the flu virus. [1]

_____

19. State what is in a vaccine that makes the vaccine effective. [1]

_____

20. Identify *one* event that could result in the virus changing to a form able to spread from human to human. [1]

_____

## Day 26

**Stop.** Check your answers and note how many correct **Points**

1. **1**    The nucleus of each cell contains a full set of chromosome, hence, all the genetic codes (DNA) of an organism.

2. **2**    Competition = two or more species of an ecosystem use the same resources for survival.

   The chipmunks and squirrels in this choice are in competition with each other because they eat the same food.

3. **1**    Two organisms are closely related if they branch off the same species in an evolutionary tree.

   Of the pairs given in each choice, only F and I evolve from (branch off) the same species (C).

4. **2**    Both A and B are the ancestors of G and C.

   But B is the most recent because it is closer to the present.

5. **4**    B is related to A, so B is similar to A.

6. **2**    In the diagram shown, a leaf captures carbon dioxide, water and sun energy, and releases oxygen.

   These substances are involved in photosynthesis.

7. **2**    Based on the diagram, the concentration of hormone B is nearly Zero on Day 2.

8. **4**    Carrying capacity = maximum population of organisms that a given ecosystem can sustain with the available resources over time.

   All resources listed are necessary to sustain life, therefore, availability of each in an ecosystem will affect the carrying capacity.

**9. 1 point**　Acceptable responses include, but are not limited to:
*Photosynthesis*
*Respiration*
*Combustion*

**10. 1 point**　Acceptable responses include, but are not limited to:
*Burning fossil fuels*
*Human population increase*
*More cars*
*More industry*
*Deforestation*

**11. 1 point**　Acceptable responses include, but are not limited to:
*Global warming*
*Increased average daily temperatures*
*Climate change*

**12. 1 point**　Acceptable responses include, but are not limited to:
*Use alternative fuels*
*Plant more trees*
*Reduce deforestation*
*Drive less*

**13. 1 point**　Acceptable responses include, but are not limited to:
*Enzymes*
*Restriction enzymes*
*Proteins*
*Biological catalysts*

14. 1 point     **The only acceptable response is the one below.**

*Electrophoresis or gel electrophoresis.*

15. 1 point     2

16. 1 point     **Acceptable responses include, but are not limited to:**

*The number of bands would differ.*

*The bands would be in different positions.*

*The banding patterns would be different.*

17. 1 point     **Acceptable responses include, but are not limited to:**

*Most flu viruses cause a runny nose and sore throat, while the H5N1 virus can cause pneumonia.*

*The avian flu goes deeper into the lungs and can cause severe pneumonia.*

*The avian flu has a more severe effect on humans than most other flu viruses.*

18. 1 point     *antibodies.*

19. 1 point     **Acceptable responses include, but are not limited to:**

*A vaccine contains dead or weakened pathogens.*

20. 1 point     **Acceptable responses include, but are not limited to:**

*Mutation*

**Start:** Answer all questions in Part A and B-1 before stopping.

**Part A:** Answer all questions in this part. [30 Points]

*Directions* (1–30): For *each* statement or question, write on your separate answer sheet the *number* of the word or expression that, of those given, best completes the statement or answers the question.

1 The greatest number of relationships between the organisms in an ecosystem is best shown in

(1) a food chain
(2) an energy pyramid
(3) a food web
(4) an ecological succession diagram

2 The diagram below shows stages of human reproduction.

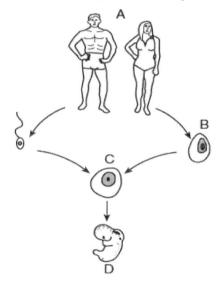

The direct result of fertilization is represented at

(1) *A*          (3) *C*
(2) *B*          (4) *D*

3 Certain organisms are able to store energy from the Sun in energy-rich compounds. Which event best illustrates this activity?

(1) A fox captures and eats a young rabbit.
(2) A caterpillar is eaten by a blackbird.
(3) Lettuce produces organic substances.
(4) Bacteria change organic material into simple nutrients.

4 The diagram below shows how a chemical message produced by one cell is received by other cells.

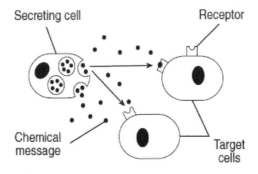

If these chemical messages are destroyed, the target cells will

(1) produce their own chemical messages
(2) not respond with appropriate actions
(3) develop different receptors
(4) no longer be produced in the organism

5 Coded instructions that are passed from one generation to the next can be most directly changed by the processes of

(1) passive transport, natural selection, and synthesis
(2) selective breeding, replication, and absorption
(3) recombination, mutation, and genetic engineering
(4) evolution, reproduction, and digestion

6 The diagram below represents a cross section of a leaf of a green plant, showing an opening (stomate) in the lower surface.

**Structure of a Leaf**

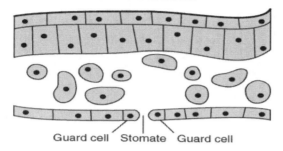

Guard cell　Stomate　Guard cell

A stomate in the lower surface of the leaf has a function most similar to the function of which cell structure?

(1) cell membrane　　　　　　　(3) ribosome
(2) vacuole　　　　　　　　　　(4) nucleus

7 When *S. marcescens*, a bacterium, is grown in a refrigerator, it produces red-colored colonies. However, if the bacterium is grown at room temperature, the colonies are white. The best explanation for this situation is that

(1) refrigeration changes the structure of genes
(2) room temperature stimulates the synthesis of a red pigment
(3) temperature has an effect on the expression of genes
(4) only temperature is responsible for the expression of a trait

8 In sexually reproducing organisms, mutations can be inherited if they occur in

(1) the egg, only
(2) the sperm, only
(3) any body cell of either the mother or the father
(4) either the egg or the sperm

9 The diagram below represents a structure found in most cells.

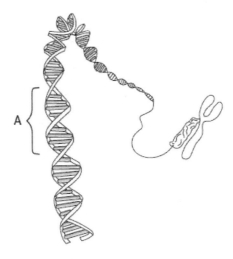

The section labeled *A* in the diagram is most likely a

(1) protein composed of folded chains of base subunits
(2) biological catalyst
(3) part of a gene for a particular trait
(4) chromosome undergoing a mutation

10 Researchers have reported that the number of different species of fish found in certain areas of the ocean has been greatly reduced over the past 50 years. This situation is an example of

(1) a loss of biodiversity
(2) an increase in ecological succession
(3) a lack of differentiation
(4) an increased carrying capacity

11 Large rebates and low-cost loans have been made available to homeowners to install solar panels to heat their homes. The use of these incentives benefits ecosystems because it

(1) encourages conservation of resources
(2) reduces the need for recycling
(3) promotes the use of nonrenewable resources
(4) discourages the use of alternative energy

12 Which sequence represents the correct order of events for the production of necessary complex molecules after food is taken in by a multicellular animal?

(1) diffusion → synthesis → absorption → digestion → circulation
(2) circulation → diffusion → synthesis → absorption → digestion
(3) digestion → absorption → circulation → diffusion → synthesis
(4) synthesis → digestion → absorption → diffusion → circulation

13 The number in each circle below represents the chromosome number of the cell. Which diagram represents the production of offspring by an asexually reproducing organism?

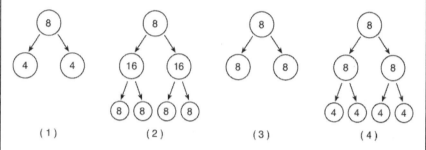

14 The arrows in the diagram below indicate the development of four different varieties of vegetable plants from wild mustard.

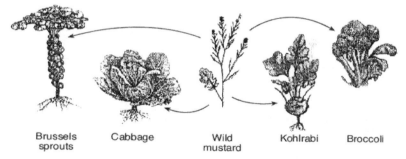

Brussels sprouts    Cabbage    Wild mustard    Kohlrabi    Broccoli

Each of these varieties was most likely produced as a result of

(1) asexual reproduction in the wild for many years
(2) changes in light availability
(3) competition between plants
(4) selective breeding over many generations

15 The sorting and recombination of genes during reproduction is important to evolution because these processes

(1) decrease variation and help maintain a stable population
(2) increase variation that enables species to adapt to change
(3) decrease the chances of producing offspring that are adapted to the environment
(4) increase the ability of all the offspring to adapt to the environment

16 A diagram of evolutionary pathways of various animal species is shown below.

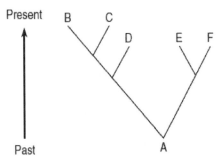

The pattern of these evolutionary pathways is most likely the result of alterations within which structure?

(1) vacuole                              (3) nucleus
(2) cell membrane                        (4) ribosome

17 Which situation is *least* likely to result in new inherited characteristics?

(1) altering genetic information
(2) changes in the structure of genes
(3) producing new individuals by means of cloning
(4) changes in the structure of individual chromosomes

18 In most mammals, the placenta is essential to the embryo for the processes of

(1) meiosis and excretion
(2) nutrition and excretion
(3) milk production and digestion
(4) blood exchange and digestion

19 Ancestors of the giant panda had rounded paws with five very short toes. Today, the giant panda has a sixth toe, often referred to as a thumb, even though it develops from a wrist bone. This unique thumb is an adaptation that allows the panda to easily hold and eat bamboo shoots. The presence of the giant panda's thumb is most likely the result of

(1) natural selection
(2) selective breeding
(3) asexual reproduction
(4) ecological succession


20 The diagram below represents levels of organization within a cell of a multicellular organism.

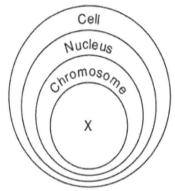

Which statement is correct regarding the structure represented by $X$?

(1) Structure $X$ is composed of many different amino acids that determine the type of cell it will become in the organism.
(2) Structure $X$ has the same base sequence in all the body cells of the organism.
(3) Structure $X$ is a folded chain arrangement of carbohydrate found in all the body cells of the organism.
(4) Structure $X$ contains 20 different kinds of subunits that are present in all the cells of the organism.


21 A pathogen passing from a mother to her fetus could cause

(1) a decrease in the chromosome number of the fetus
(2) an increase in milk production in the mother
(3) gamete production to increase
(4) an infection in the fetus

22 The diagram below represents the human male reproductive system.

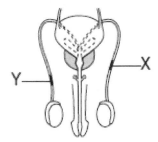

Which activity would be prevented by blockages at *X* and *Y*?

(1) transport of urine out of the body
(2) passage of testosterone to the female to stimulate egg production
(3) movement of sperm out of the body
(4) movement of testosterone to the testes to stimulate sperm production

23 One environmental problem caused by the use of nuclear power as an energy source is the

(1) destruction of the ozone shield
(2) disposal of wastes
(3) production of acid rain
(4) accumulation of $CO_2$ in the atmosphere

24 Which method of protecting members of an endangered species is most ecologically sound?

(1) protecting the habitats where these animals live from human development
(2) capturing these animals and putting them in wildlife parks
(3) feeding and constructing shelters for these organisms
(4) passing laws that encourage hunting of the predators of these species

25 The interaction of which two systems provides the molecules needed for the metabolic activity that takes place at ribosomes?

(1) digestive and circulatory
(2) reproductive and excretory
(3) immune and nervous
(4) respiratory and muscular

26 The swordfish contains a heat generating organ that warms its brain and eyes up to 14°C above the surrounding ocean water temperature. Which structures are most likely to be found at relatively high concentrations within the cells of this heat generating organ?

(1) nuclei
(2) chloroplasts
(3) chromosomes
(4) mitochondria

27 Two species of animals with a similar appearance live in the same habitat but do *not* compete for food. This is because they most likely

(1) reproduce at different times of the year
(2) are the same size
(3) occupy different ecological niches
(4) are active at night

28 During its annual migration, the red knot, a medium-size shorebird, flies the entire length of North and South America. During one critical stop to feed on the eggs of horseshoe crabs, the birds nearly double their body mass. The relationship between the red knot and the horseshoe crab is that of

(1) parasite–host
(2) consumer–producer
(3) scavenger–producer
(4) predator–prey

29 It is recommended that people at risk for serious flu complications be vaccinated so that their bodies will produce
(1) antigens to fight the flu virus
(2) antibodies against the flu virus
(3) toxins to fight the infection caused by the flu virus
(4) antibiotics to reduce symptoms caused by the flu virus

30 The diagram below represents a process that occurs during normal human development.

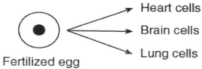

Which statement is correct regarding the cells and DNA?
(1) All the cells have identical DNA.
(2) The DNA of the fertilized egg differs from the DNA of all the other cells.
(3) The DNA of the fertilized egg differs from some, but not all, of the other cells.
(4) Only the fertilized egg contains DNA.

## Part B–1: Answer all questions in this part. (15 points)

*Directions* (31–45): For *each* statement or question, write on the separate answer sheet the *number* of the word or expression that, of those given, best completes the statement or answers the question.

31 Activities in the human body are represented in the diagram below.

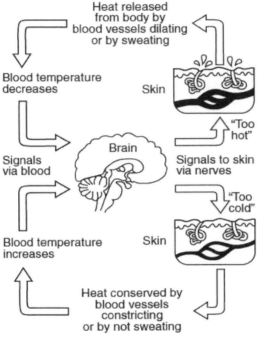

Heat released
from body by
blood vessels dilating
or by sweating

Blood temperature
decreases

Skin

"Too
hot"

Brain

Signals
via blood

Signals to skin
via nerves

"Too
cold"

Blood temperature
increases

Skin

Heat conserved by
blood vessels
constricting
or by not sweating

(Not drawn to scale)

Source: Campbell and Reece,
*Biology*, 6th edition (adapted)

Which title would be appropriate for the diagram?

(1) Rate of Excretion Varies in Response to Amount of Water Taken In
(2) Feedback Mechanisms Help to Maintain Homeostasis
(3) Respiratory Rate Responds to an Increase in Muscle Activity
(4) The Nervous System Responds to Changes in Blood Sugar Levels

32 A company that manufactures a popular multivitamin wanted to determine whether their multivitamin had any side effects. For its initial study, the company chose 2000 individuals to take one of their multivitamin tablets per day for one year. Scientists from the company surveyed the participants to determine whether they had experienced any side effects. The greatest problem with this procedure is that

(1) only one brand of vitamin was tested
(2) the study lasted only one year
(3) the sample size was not large enough
(4) no control group was used

33 In a particular ecosystem, squirrels make up a large portion of the diet of coyotes. A fatal disease in the squirrel population begins to reduce their population over a period of months. Which graph best represents the expected changes in population size of the coyotes and the squirrels?

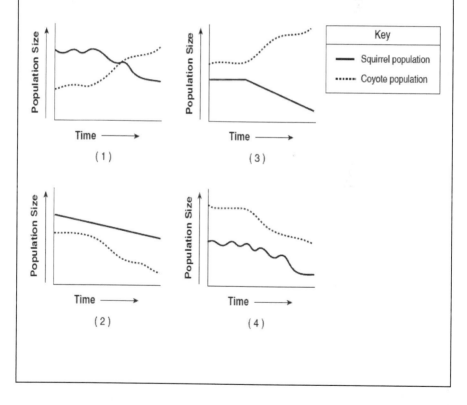

34 Which statement would most likely be used to describe the procedure represented in the diagram below?

Bacterial
DNA

Human
insulin
gene

(1) Enzymes are used to assemble an insulin gene, which is then attached to bacterial DNA.

(2) Bacterial DNA is cut from a human DNA strand and inserted into a human cell to form an insulin gene.

(3) The insulin gene is cut out of a human DNA strand using an enzyme and inserted into bacterial DNA, resulting in a combination of different DNA segments.

(4) A gene is deleted from bacterial DNA to produce an insulin gene, which is then inserted into human DNA.

35 Part of a molecule found in cells is represented below.

Which process is most directly affected by the arrangement of components 1 through 4?

(1) diffusion through cell membranes

(2) fertilization of a sex cell

(3) sequencing of amino acids in cells

(4) increasing the number of cells in an organism

36 What is the volume of water represented in the graduated cylinder shown below?

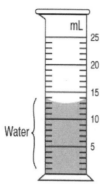

(1) 10.3 mL

(2) 13.0 mL

(3) 14.0 mL

(4) 15.0 mL

37 A student prepared a test tube containing yeast, glucose, and water. After 24 hours, the test tube was analyzed for the presence of several substances. What substance would the student expect to find if respiration occurred in the test tube?

(1) a hormone

(2) starch

(3) nitrogen

(4) carbon dioxide

38 A student used the low-power objective of a compound light microscope and observed a single-celled organism as shown in the diagram below.

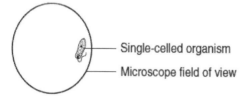

When he switched to high power, the organism was no longer visible. This most likely happened because switching to high power made the

(1) field too bright to see the organism

(2) image too small to be seen

(3) area of the slide being viewed smaller

(4) fine-adjustment knob no longer functional

39 The daphnia shown below has produced three egg cells, eats live single-celled organisms, lives in freshwater, and is caught and eaten by animals known as hydra.

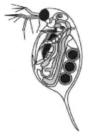

Which terms would most likely be used in a description of this organism?

(1) asexual reproduction, herbivore, prey, aquatic, heterotrophic
(2) sexual reproduction, predator, aquatic, heterotrophic, prey
(3) asexual reproduction, autotrophic, predator, terrestrial, scavenger
(4) sexual reproduction, carnivore, aquatic, autotrophic, prey

40 Changes in a deer population are shown in the graph below.

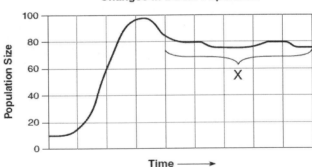

Which statement best explains section $X$?

(1) The population has reached the carrying capacity of its environment.
(2) Energy is used for interbreeding between members of different species.
(3) A predator recycles the remains of dead organisms.
(4) Competition does not occur between members of different species in the same habitat.

41 The diagram below shows various ecological communities that occupied an area over a period of 300 years.

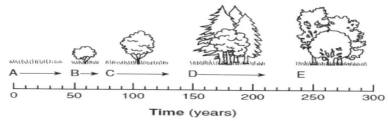

**Time (years)**

Which statement best describes the diagram?

(1) Community *A* is the most stable community.
(2) Community *B* replaced community *C* after a period of 100 years.
(3) Community *C* developed into community *A* after a period of 75 years.
(4) Community *D* modified the environment, making it more suitable for community *E*.

Base your answers to questions 42 and 43 on the food web below and on your knowledge of biology.

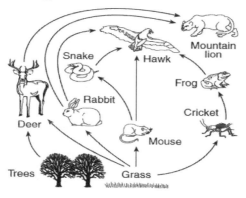

42 Which organisms are carnivores?

(1) grass and trees                    (3) deer and mountain lion
(2) mouse, rabbit, and cricket         (4) frog, snake, and hawk

43 A *decrease* in the grass population will most immediately *decrease* the available energy for the

(1) mouse                              (3) snake
(2) hawk                               (4) frog

44 The diagram below shows two different kinds of substances, *A* and *B*, entering a cell. ATP is most likely being used for

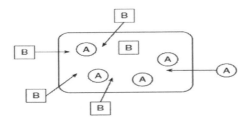

(1) substance *A* to enter the cell
(2) substance *B* to enter the cell

(3) both substances to enter the cell
(4) neither substance to enter the cell

45 A biological process that occurs in plants is represented below.

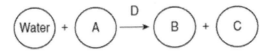

Which row in the chart below identifies the lettered substances in this process?

| Row | A | B | C | D |
|-----|-----|-----|-----|-----|
| (1) | enzymes | oxygen | carbon dioxide | glucose |
| (2) | carbon dioxide | glucose | oxygen | enzymes |
| (3) | glucose | enzymes | oxygen | carbon dioxide |
| (4) | oxygen | glucose | carbon dioxide | enzymes |

**Day 27**

**Stop.** Check your answers and note how many correct **Points**

# Day 27          Answers

## Part A

| | | |
|---|---|---|
| 1) 3 | 11) 1 | 21) 4 |
| 2) 3 | 12) 3 | 22) 3 |
| 3) 3 | 13) 3 | 23) 2 |
| 4) 2 | 14) 4 | 24) 1 |
| 5) 3 | 15) 2 | 25) 1 |
| 6) 1 | 16) 3 | 26) 4 |
| 7) 3 | 17) 3 | 27) 3 |
| 8) 4 | 18) 2 | 28) 4 |
| 9) 3 | 19) 1 | 29) 2 |
| 10) 1 | 20) 2 | 30) 1 |

## Part B-1

| | |
|---|---|
| 31) 2 | 39) 2 |
| 32) 4 | 40) 1 |
| 33) 2 | 41) 4 |
| 34) 3 | 42) 4 |
| 35) 3 | 43) 1 |
| 36) 2 | 44) 1 |
| 37) 4 | 45) 2 |
| 38) 3 | |

Start:  Answer all questions in B-2, C and D before stopping.

Part B–2:  Answer all questions in this part. (10 point)
*Directions* (46–55): For those questions that are followed by four choices, circle the *number* preceding the choice that, of those given, best completes the statement or answers the question. For all other questions in

*Base your answers to questions 46 through 50 on the data table below and on your knowledge of biology. The data table shows the concentrations of oxygen in parts per million (ppm) present in freshwater and seawater at various temperatures.*

Concentration of Oxygen in Water

| Temperature (°C) | Oxygen Concentration in Freshwater (ppm) | Oxygen Concentration in Seawater (ppm) |
|------------------|------------------------------------------|----------------------------------------|
| 1 | 14.0 | 11.0 |
| 10 | 11.5 | 9.0 |
| 15 | 10.0 | 8.0 |
| 20 | 9.0 | 7.5 |
| 25 | 8.0 | 7.0 |
| 30 | 7.5 | 6.0 |

*Directions* (46–48): Using the information in the data table, construct a line graph on the grid on the next page, following the directions below.

46 Mark an appropriate scale on each labeled axis. [1]

47 Plot the data for freshwater oxygen concentration on the grid. Surround each point with a small circle and connect the points. [1]

Example:

48 Plot the data for seawater oxygen concentration on the grid. Surround each point with a small triangle and connect the points. [1]

Example:

## Concentration of Oxygen in Water

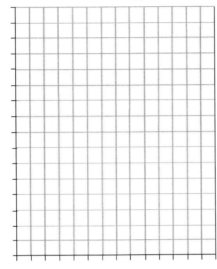

Oxygen Concentration (ppm)

Temperature (°C)

| Key | |
|---|---|
| ⊙ | Oxygen in freshwater |
| △ | Oxygen in seawater |

49 Predict the oxygen concentration in freshwater at 35°C. [1]

_____ **ppm**

50 State *one* relationship between temperature and dissolved oxygen concentration in water. [1]

_____

_____

Base your answers to questions 51 through 53 on the passage below and on your knowledge of biology.

### A New Theory on Malaria Transmission

*Plasmodium falciparum*, one parasite that causes malaria, spreads rapidly, infecting up to 500 million people every year. Malaria spreads when an infected mosquito bites an uninfected human, who then becomes infected. This infected human is bitten by an uninfected mosquito, which then becomes infected. This infected mosquito then bites and infects an uninfected human. Malaria transmission is illustrated below.

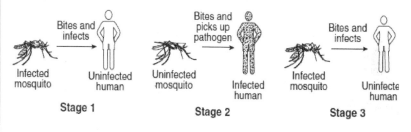

(Not drawn to scale)

Scientists have a new idea about how this disease spreads. When the malaria parasite is passed to humans through the bite of an infected mosquito, there is a great possibility that this action alters the chemical scent of the human. The altered human body scent then attracts more uninfected mosquitoes, which bite the infected person, thus spreading the disease.

To test this hypothesis, an experiment was conducted on humans infected with malaria. The results indicate that malaria gametocytes (a stage of the parasite) may trigger the production of chemicals that change the scent of the human. The change in human scent makes humans more appealing to mosquitoes.

Scientists are now studying ways to copy this chemical scent for use in traps that would attract mosquitoes.

51 Which statement best describes the role of gametocytes in the spread o
   malaria?
   (1) They give off a scent that attracts infected mosquitoes.
   (2) They absorb human body scents that attract mosquitoes.
   (3) They release a scent into the human body.
   (4) They cause a chemical reaction that alters human scent.

52 Malaria is easily spread because uninfected mosquitoes are attracted to
   (1) humans without malaria
   (2) humans infected with gametocytes
   (3) gametocytes in other mosquitoes
   (4) mosquitoes that are uninfected

53 State *one* reason why the use of synthetic scents in traps is a better way to
   lower mosquito populations than spraying with pesticides. [1]

   _____

   _____

*Base your answers to questions 54 and 55 on the information below and on
your knowledge of biology.*

   The graph below shows the effect of substrate concentration on the
   action of enzyme *X*. This enzyme is functioning at its optimal
   temperature, 36°C, and at its optimal pH, 5.5.

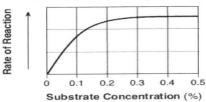

**Effect of Substrate Concentration
on the Rate of Enzyme Action**

54 When the substrate concentration increases from 0.4% to 0.5%, the rate of the
   reaction
   (1) decreases                    (3) remains the same
   (2) increases                    (4) increases, then decreases

55 State what would most likely happen to the rate of enzyme action if the
   temperature were reduced by 10 degrees. Support your answer. [1]

   _____

## Part C:   Answer all questions in this part. (17 points)

*Directions* (56–67): Record your answers in the spaces provided in this examination booklet.

*Base your answers to questions 56 and 57 on the experimental setup shown below. The tubing connected to both flask setups used in the experiment provides oxygen to the solution.*

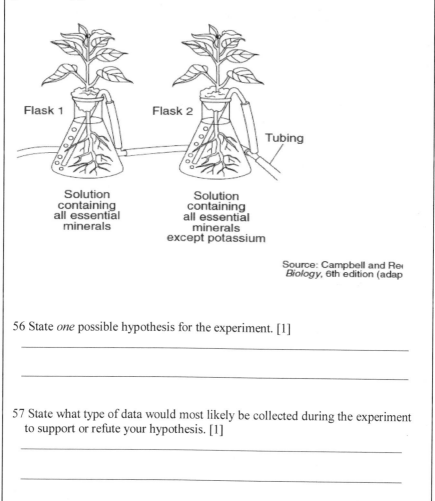

Flask 1

Flask 2

Tubing

Solution
containing
all essential
minerals

Solution
containing
all essential
minerals
except potassium

Source: Campbell and Ree
*Biology*, 6th edition (adap

56 State *one* possible hypothesis for the experiment. [1]

_____

_____

57 State what type of data would most likely be collected during the experiment to support or refute your hypothesis. [1]

_____

_____

*Base your answer to question 58 on the information below and on your knowledge of biology.*

Stem cells present in an embryo are responsible for the formation of various tissues and organs. Recent research suggests that it may be possible to replicate stem cells from sections of skin taken from adult mice, rather than having to use stem cells from the embryos of mice. In the future, human stem cells may be used to replace human tissue damaged by diseases such as Parkinson's disease and multiple sclerosis.

58 Discuss why the use of stem cells taken from a patient to replace damaged tissues and organs may decrease the potential risk to a patient. In your answer, be sure to:

• identify the major problem that may occur when tissues and organs donated by another individual are used [1]
• explain why this problem may occur [1]
• explain why this problem will *not* occur if tissues and organs produced by stem cells from the patient are used [1]

59 *Staphylococcus aureus* is a type of bacterium that lives on the skin and in the nostrils of most people. Generally, it is controlled by the immune system of the body. Occasionally, the antibiotic penicillin is needed to control the bacterium.

However, some strains of *S. aureus* have a resistance to penicillin, which makes them hard to kill and infections difficult to cure.

Explain how the resistance to penicillin affects the *S. aureus* population. In your answer, be sure to include an explanation of:

• how the exposure to penicillin affects the survival of some bacteria in the population [1]
• why the frequency of penicillin-resistant bacteria can change over time within the population [1]
• how it is still possible to cure patients who are infected with penicillin-resistant bacteria [1]

_____

_____

_____

_____

_____

_____

*Base your answers to questions 60 through 63 on the information below and on your knowledge of biology.*

An ecology class is trying to help reduce the problem of global warming by asking their school district to change all of their old light bulbs to compact fluorescent light bulbs that use less electricity.

60 Identify *one* specific gas that contributes to the problem of global warming. [1]

_____

61 State *one* activity of humans that increases the concentration of this gas. [1]

_____

62 Describe *one negative* effect of global warming on humans or ecosystems. [1]

_____

_____

63 Explain why switching to more efficient light bulbs will help reduce the school's contribution to global warming. [1]

_____

_____

*Base your answers to questions 64 and 65 on the information below and on your knowledge of biology.*

### There's No Place Like Home!

Some pets need expensive food, or grow to large sizes, or have nasty, dangerous behavior. Because of this, some people realize that they can no longer care for their pets. A pet twist-neck turtle in a state of near starvation was found by rescuers at the Brooklyn Botanic Garden. The food that this species eats is not commonly found in New York State. In Florida and other warm states, people have released pet snakes such as pythons and anacondas into local lakes and swamps, where they have become a threat to other animals and even to humans. Those released pets that survive in their new environment can eventually breed and multiply, causing even more problems!

64 Identify *one* abiotic factor that might affect the survival of a released pet and explain why that factor would affect survival. [1]

_____

_____

65 State *one* reason released pets that survive in a new environment may be able to form a large population. [1]

_____

_____

*Base your answers to questions 66 and 67 on the information and diagrams below and on your knowledge of biology.*

There are over 40 different species of butterfly fish found in tropical reefs throughout the world. Three different species of butterfly fish are shown below.

Fish A                  Fish B                  Fish C

The fish fin diagram and dichotomous key shown below can be used to determine the species of each of these fish.

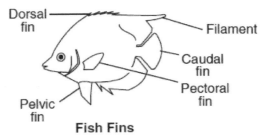

**Fish Fins**

| Dichotomous Key to Butterfly Fish | |
|---|---|
| 1. a. Pelvic fin dark | 2 |
|    b. Pelvic fin light | 4 |
| 2. a. Two large white spots below dorsal fin | C. quadrimacul |
|    b. Lacks two large white spots below dorsal fin | 3 |
| 3. a. Caudal fin with two dark bars at tip | C. reticulatus |
|    b. Caudal fin with one dark bar at tip | C. kleinii |
| 4. a. Dorsal fin has long filament extension | 5 |
|    b. Filament extension lacking from dorsal fin | 6 |
| 5. a. Large dark spot on body near filament | C. ephippium |
|    b. Small dark spot on body near filament | C. auriga |
| 6. a ... | |

*Directions* (66–67): Using the information and dichotomous key, complete the table following the directions below.

66 Use the dichotomous key and fish fin diagram to identify fish *A*, *B*, and *C* and write the name of *each* fish in the column labeled "Scientific Name" in the table below. [1]

67 Select *two* characteristics from the dichotomous key that are useful for determining the identity of fish *A*, *B*, and *C*. Using these characteristics, label the headings for the last two columns in the table and complete the last two columns in the table. [2]

| Fish | Scientific Name | Subgroup | | |
|---|---|---|---|---|
| A | | Rabdophorus | | |
| B | | Lepidochaetodon | | |
| C | | Rabdophorus | | |

**Part D:** Answer all questions in this part. [13 Points]

*Directions* (68–78): For those questions that are followed by four choices, circle the *number* of the choice that, of those given, best completes the statement or answers the question. For all other questions in this part,

*Base your answer to question 68 on the chart below and on your knowledge of biology.*

### Universal Genetic Code Chart
### Messenger RNA and the Amino Acids for Which They Code

|  | U | C | A | G |  |
|---|---|---|---|---|---|
| **U** | UUU UUC } PHE<br>UUA UUG } LEU | UCU UCC UCA UCG } SER | UAU UAC } TYR<br>UAA UAG } STOP | UGU UGC } CYS<br>UGA } STOP<br>UGG } TRP | U C A G |
| **C** | CUU CUC CUA CUG } LEU | CCU CCC CCA CCG } PRO | CAU CAC } HIS<br>CAA CAG } GLN | CGU CGC CGA CGG } ARG | U C A G |
| **A** | AUU AUC AUA } ILE<br>AUG } MET or START | ACU ACC ACA ACG } THR | AAU AAC } ASN<br>AAA AAG } LYS | AGU AGC } SER<br>AGA AGG } ARG | U C A G |
| **G** | GUU GUC GUA GUG } VAL | GCU GCC GCA GCG } ALA | GAU GAC } ASP<br>GAA GAG } GLU | GGU GGC GGA GGG } GLY | U C A G |

68 Fill in the missing mRNA bases and the amino acid sequence that corresponds to the DNA base sequence below. [2]

| **DNA** | CAC | GTG | GAC | TGA |
|---|---|---|---|---|
| **mRNA** | _____ | _____ | _____ | _____ |
| **Amino acids** | _____ | _____ | _____ | _____ |

*Base your answers to questions 69 and 70 on the information below and on your knowledge of biology.*

An investigation is carried out to determine the effect of exercise on the rate at which a person can squeeze a clothespin.

69 In this investigation, the independent variable is the

(1) control
(2) exercise
(3) rate of squeezing
(4) number of participants

70 Muscle fatigue occurs during this activity when

(1) carbon dioxide is used up in the muscle cells
(2) simple sugar is converted to starch in the muscle cells
(3) proteins accumulate in mitochondria in the muscle cells
(4) certain waste products collect in the muscle cells

71 Part of a laboratory procedure is shown in the diagram below.

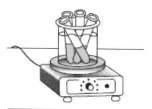

This setup would most likely be involved in a procedure to

(1) stain specimens while making a wet mount
(2) test for the presence of glucose using an indicator
(3) separate pigments in a mixture
(4) determine the pH of solutions

*Base your answers to questions 72 and 73 on the information below and on your knowledge of biology.*

A valuable medicine is obtained from a certain rare species of plant. Scientists are anxious to find another more abundant species of plant that is closely related to the rare one, and also produces the medicine.

Two newly discovered plant species, *A* and *B*, were studied and compared   the rare one. The results of the study are shown in the table below.

| Species of Plant | Characteristics of Flowers | Shape of Leaves | Species Number of Chromosomes | Enzyme A Present | Enzyme B Present | Enzyme C Present |
|---|---|---|---|---|---|---|
| rare species | pink 5 petals | round | 36 | yes | yes | yes |
| species A | pink 5 petals | oval | 34 | no | no | yes |
| species B | white 5 petals | round | 36 | yes | yes | yes |

72 Which newly discovered species is more closely related to the rare species? Support  your answer. [1]

Species:_____

_____

_____

73 Which procedure could also be carried out to help determine which newly discovered species is most closely related to the rare species?

(1) measurement of respiration rate in the plants
(2) chromatography of pigment extracts from the plants
(3) determination of the type of gas released by photosynthesis in the plants
(4) analysis of chemical bonds present in glucose in the plants

74 The characteristics of four finches that inhabit the same island are represented in the chart below.

### Characteristics Chart

| Large Ground Finch | Warbler Finch |
|---|---|
| Beak: crushing<br>Food: mainly plant | Beak: probing<br>Food: 100% animal |
| **Small Ground Finch** | **Large Tree Finch** |
| Beak: crushing<br>Food: mainly plant | Beak: grasping<br>Food: mainly animal |

Complete the table below using information in the characteristics chart and your knowledge of biology. [2]

| Competes With the Large Tree Finch | Type of Finch | State *one* reason why it competes *or* does *not* compete with the large tree finch. |
|---|---|---|
| no | | |
| yes | | |

75 Studies of the finches of the Galapagos Islands have shown that

(1) DNA will change to produce structures needed by birds to survive intense competition
(2) a bird's beak changes annually in response to the type of food that is most abundant each year
(3) natural selection occurs when there are scarce resources and intense competition
(4) the beak of a finch will change if the environment of the bird remains stable

*Base your answers to questions 76 through 78 on the information below and on your knowledge of biology.*

A student prepared four different red blood cell suspensions, as shown in the chart below.

| Suspension | Contents |
|------------|----------|
| A | red blood cells in normal blood serum (0.7% salt solution) |
| B | red blood cells in 10% salt solution |
| C | red blood cells in distilled water |
| D | red blood cells in tap water |

76 Which suspension would contain red blood cells that would appear wrinkled and reduced in volume?

(1) *A*                                    (3) *C*
(2) *B*                                    (4) *D*

77 The change in red blood cell volume is principally due to the movement of

(1) serum                                  (3) water
(2) oxygen                                 (4) salt

78 Which process is most likely involved in the change in red blood cell volume?

(1) active transport                       (3) replication
(2) evaporation                            (4) diffusion

**Day 28**

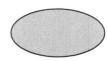

**Stop.** Check your answers and note how many correct **Points**

## Part B-2

46. **1 point**   For marking an appropriate scale on each axis.

47. **1 point**   For correctly plotting freshwater data, surrounding each point with a small circle, and connecting the points.

48. **1 point**   For correctly plotting seawater data, surrounding each point with a small triangle, and connecting the points.

Example of a 3-credit response to questions 46–48:

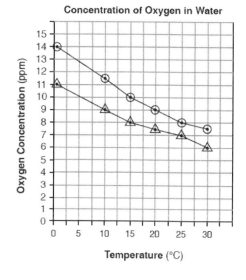

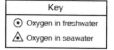

49. **1 point**   For response between **6 ppm and 7.5 ppm.**

50. **1 point**   **Acceptable responses include, but are not limited to:**

*As temperature increases, oxygen concentration decreases.*

*As temperature decreases, oxygen concentration increases.*

51. **1 point**　　*4*

52. **1 point**　　*2*

53. **1 point**　　**Acceptable responses include, but are not limited to:**

*The scents are very specific for the insect they attract.*

*Pesticides disrupt food webs.*

*Pesticides affect organisms other than mosquitoes.*

*Over time, more insects that are resistant to the pesticide would appear in the population.*

54. **1 point**　　*3*

55. **1 point**　　**Acceptable responses include, but are not limited to:**

*The reaction will slow down because it is below the optimal temperature.*

## Part C

56. **1 point**　　**Acceptable responses include, but are not limited to:**

*Potassium helps plants grow.*

*Potassium is not needed by plants for proper growth.*

*Plants missing potassium will not grow tall.*

*Plants lacking potassium will not be green.*

**Note:** Do *not* allow credit for a hypothesis written in the form of a question.

57. **1 point.**   **Acceptable responses include, but are not limited to:**

*Plant height*

*Number/size of leaves/roots*

*Amount/percent of leaf discoloration*

*Daily growth*

**Note:** The type of data must be measurable. Allow credit for an answer consistent with the student's hypothesis.

58. **3 points**   **Acceptable responses for each point category include, but are not limited to what are listed:**

*Identifying the major problem that may occur when tissues and organs donated by another individual are used.* **(1 point)**

*Rejection of tissues or organs*

*Explaining why this problem may occur.* **(1 point)**

*Foreign proteins from donated/tissues/organs trigger immune response*

*Immune system attacks foreign tissues/organs*

*Explaining why this problem will not occur if tissues and organs produced by stem cells from the patient are used.* **(1 point)**

*Proteins in tissues/organs will be the same as those of the patient, so the immune system will not attack.*

59. **3 points**    Acceptable responses for each point category include, but are not limited to what are listed:

***Explaining how the exposure to penicillin affects the survival of some bacteria in the population.* ( 1 point)**

*Bacteria may vary in their susceptibility to penicillin, and resistant ones survive.*

*In the bacteria that survive, there are naturally occurring variations that provide resistance to penicillin.*

*When exposed to penicillin, more of the resistant ones survive.*

*Nonresistant bacteria die off.*

***Explaining why the frequency of penicillin-resistant bacteria can change over time within the population.* (1 point)**

*When exposed to penicillin, the frequency of resistant bacteria will increase as those that are resistant survive and reproduce.*

*The resistant bacteria will survive and they will produce offspring that are resistant.*

***Explaining how it is still possible to cure patients who are infected with penicillin-resistant bacteria.* (1 point)**

*Patients can be treated with antibiotics other than penicillin.*

60. **1 point**    **Acceptable responses include, but are not limited to:**
*Carbon dioxide ($CO_2$)*

*Methane ($CH_4$)*

*Nitrous oxide*

*CFCs*

61. **1 point**     **Acceptable responses include, but are not limited to:**

**Carbon dioxide:**
*burning fossil fuels*

*deforestation*

*driving cars*

**Methane:**
*establishing landfills*

*raising cattle*

**Nitrous oxide:**
*treating raw sewage*

*producing synthetic fertilizers*

**CFCs:**
*air conditioner leaks*

*use of certain aerosols*

62. **1 point**     **Acceptable responses include, but are not limited to:**

*higher sea levels*

*habitat loss*

*climate change*

63. **1 point**     **Acceptable responses include, but are not limited to:**

*They would use less electricity, resulting in less fossil fuels being burned.*

*Reduced energy use would decrease the amount of fossil fuels burned.*

**64. 1 point**     **Acceptable responses include, but are not limited to:**

*Lack of water could result in dehydration, which interferes with cell functions.*

*Temperature, because different species are adapted to live in different climates*

**65. 1 point**     **Acceptable responses include, but are not limited to:**

*Lack of natural predators*

*Food/prey may be extremely abundant in the new environment.*

*Breed and multiply in the new environment*

**66. 1 point**     **For Identifying fish A, B, and C and writing the name of each fish in the column labeled "Scientific Name" in the table.**

**Note:** Allow this credit even if the genus (*C.*) is *not* included.

**67. 2 point**     **For selecting *two* characteristics from the dichotomous key** that are useful for determining the identity of fish *A*, *B*, and *C* and labeling the headings for the last two columns in the table. **(1 point)**

For **correctly completing the last two columns in the table. (1 point)**

**Example of a 3-point response for 66 and 67:**

| Fish | Scientific Name | Subgroup | Pelvic Fin Color | Spot Near Dorsal Fin Filament |
|------|-----------------|----------|------------------|-------------------------------|
| A | *C. ephippium* | Rabdophorus | light | large |
| B | *C. kleinii* | Lepidochaetodon | dark | none |
| C | *C. auriga* | Rabdophorus | light | small |

68. **2 points**   **1 point** for correctly filling in the missing mRNA bases.

**1 point** for correctly filling in the amino acid sequence corresponding to the DNA sequences

**Example of a 2-credit response:**

| DNA | CAC | GTG | GAC | TGA |
|---|---|---|---|---|
| **mRNA** | GUG | CAC | CUG | ACU |
| **Amino acids** | VAL | HIS | LEU | THR |

**Note:** Allow credit for an amino acid sequence that is consistent with the student's response for the mRNA sequence.

69. **1 point**   2

70. **1 point**   4

71. **1 point**   2

72. **1 point**   *Species B* **and** for supporting the answer.

**Acceptable explanation include, but are not limited to:**

*because it has more characteristics in common with the rare species*

73. **1 point**   2

74. **2 points**    Allow 1 credit for completing *both* columns for each of the finches.

**Example of a 2-credit response:**

| Competes With the Large Tree Finch | Type of Finch | State *one* reason why it competes *or* does *not* compete with the large tree finch. |
|---|---|---|
| no | large/small ground finch *or* warbler finch | The large tree finch eats mainly animal food, while the large/small ground finch eats mainly plant food. *or* The warbler finch may eat different animals. |
| yes | warbler finch | They both eat animal food. |

75. **1 point**    3

76. **1 point**    2

77. **1 point**    3

78. **1 point**    4

## 1. Your Raw Score: _____

Add your day 27 and day 28 points .

## 2. Your Regents Grade: _____

Use the conversion chart below. The Scale Score corresponding to your Raw Score is your Regents Grade for this exam.

| Raw Score | Scale Score | Raw Score | Scale Score | Raw Score | Scale Score |
|---|---|---|---|---|---|
| 85 | 100 | 56 | 77 | 27 | 52 |
| 84 | 98 | 55 | 77 | 26 | 50 |
| 83 | 97 | 54 | 76 | 25 | 49 |
| 82 | 96 | 53 | 75 | 24 | 48 |
| 81 | 95 | 52 | 75 | 23 | 46 |
| 80 | 94 | 51 | 74 | 22 | 45 |
| 79 | 93 | 50 | 73 | 21 | 43 |
| 78 | 92 | 49 | 73 | 20 | 42 |
| 77 | 92 | 48 | 72 | 19 | 40 |
| 76 | 91 | 47 | 71 | 18 | 39 |
| 75 | 90 | 46 | 70 | 17 | 37 |
| 74 | 89 | 45 | 70 | 16 | 35 |
| 73 | 88 | 44 | 69 | 15 | 34 |
| 72 | 88 | 43 | 68 | 14 | 32 |
| 71 | 87 | 42 | 67 | 13 | 30 |
| 70 | 86 | 41 | 66 | 12 | 28 |
| 69 | 86 | 40 | 66 | 11 | 26 |
| 68 | 85 | 39 | 65 | 10 | 24 |
| 67 | 84 | 38 | 64 | 9 | 22 |
| 66 | 84 | 37 | 63 | 8 | 20 |
| 65 | 83 | 36 | 62 | 7 | 18 |
| 64 | 82 | 35 | 61 | 6 | 16 |
| 63 | 82 | 34 | 60 | 5 | 13 |
| 62 | 81 | 33 | 59 | 4 | 11 |
| 61 | 80 | 32 | 57 | 3 | 8 |
| 60 | 80 | 31 | 56 | 2 | 6 |
| 59 | 79 | 30 | 55 | 1 | 3 |
| 58 | 79 | 29 | 54 | 0 | 0 |
| 57 | 78 | 28 | 53 | | |

**Start:** Answer all questions in Part A and B-1 before stopping.

**Part A:** Answer all questions in this part. [30 Points]

*Directions* (1–30): For *each* statement or question, write on your separate answer sheet the *number* of the word or expression that, of those given, best completes the statement or answers the question.

---

1 Which phrase is an example of autotrophic nutrition?

(1) a cow eating grass in a field
(2) a mushroom digesting a dead log
(3) an apple tree making its own food
(4) a tapeworm feeding in the body of a dog

2 The ability of estrogen to affect certain cells depends directly on

(1) amino acids          (3) gametes
(2) receptor molecules   (4) nerve cells

3 By studying the chemicals in rare plants that grow only in rain forests, scientists hope to discover new life-saving medicines. Chances of finding such new medicines are reduced by

(1) predation by carnivores
(2) homeostasis in organisms
(3) recycling of materials in food webs
(4) loss of species due to human activities

4 When a species includes organisms with a wide variety of traits, it is most likely that this species will have

(1) a high proportion of individuals immune to genetic diseases
(2) a greater chance to survive if environmental conditions suddenly change
(3) less success competing for resources
(4) limitless supplies of important resources, such as food and water

5 Some diseases and their causes are listed below.
　　　　　A. Flu—influenza virus
　　　　　B. Lung cancer—smoking
　　　　　C. Cystic fibrosis—genes
　　　　　D. Dysentery—parasitic ameba

Which disease would individuals have the greatest difficulty preventing in themselves?

(1) *A*          (3) *C*
(2) *B*          (4) *D*

---

6 The diagram below represents the banding pattern for human chromosome 11, with some of the bands labeled.

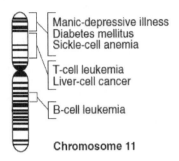

**Chromosome 11**

The bands represent
(1) proteins          (3) starches
(2) genes             (4) enzymes

7 A liver cell can make enzymes that a heart cell can *not* make because liver cells

(1) digest large, complex molecules
(2) contain more DNA than heart cells
(3) use different genes than the heart cells use
(4) remove carbon dioxide from blood

8 As male children get older, some begin to closely resemble their fathers and have no resemblance to their mothers. Which statement best explains this observation?

(1) Several sperm fertilized the egg, so the fertilized egg contained more genes from their father.
(2) More genes are inherited from the sperm cell of their father than from the cell of their mother, so most traits will be like those of their father.
(3) More genes from their father are expressed in traits that can be seen, and more genes from their mother are expressed in traits that cannot be seen, such as blood type or enzyme function.
(4) Genes from their father are stronger than genes from their mother, so the

9 Which row in the chart below contains a cell structure paired with its primary function?

| Row | Cell Structure | Function |
|-----|----------------|----------|
| (1) | ribosome | protein synthesis |
| (2) | vacuole | production of genetic information |
| (3) | nucleus | carbohydrate synthesis |
| (4) | mitochondrion | waste disposal |

10 Which sequence represents the levels of biological organization from smallest to largest?

(1) organism → cell → tissue → organelle → organ system → organ
(2) organ system → organ → organism → cell → tissue → organelle
(3) organelle → organ system → cell → organism → tissue → organ
(4) organelle → cell → tissue → organ → organ system → organism

11 The diagram below represents division of a cell that produces two daughter cells.

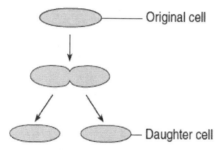

Which statement most likely describes the daughter cells produced?

(1) The daughter cells will pass on only half of the genetic information they received from the original cell.
(2) The daughter cells will each produce offspring that will have the same genetic information as the original cell.
(3) The daughter cells will each undergo the same mutations as the original cell after reproduction has occurred.
(4) The daughter cells will not pass on any of the genes that they received from the original cell.

12 Which concept is best represented in the diagram below?

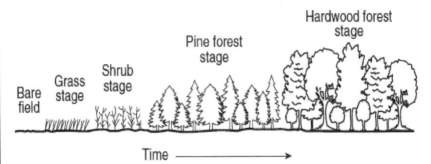

Time ⟶

(1) random mutations
(2) ecological succession

(3) genetic engineering
(4) direct harvesting

13 The cells that make up leaves on a tree are genetically identical, yet the leaves often have different shapes and sizes, as shown in the diagram below.

**Leaves of White Oak** *(Quercus alba)*

Top leaves        Bottom leaves

Which statement best explains this difference in leaf appearance?

(1) The leaves at the top of the tree get more sunlight, causing the genes in their cells to be expressed differently.
(2) The genes in the cells of leaves at the top of the tree are destroyed by sunlight, causing the leaves to stop growing.
(3) The leaves near the bottom of the tree have more genes related to leaf size, causing them to grow larger.
(4) The genes in the cells of leaves near the bottom of the tree increase in number, causing them to grow even larger.

14 Selective breeding is a technique that is used to

(1) give all organisms a chance to reproduce
(2) produce organisms from extinct species
(3) produce offspring with certain desirable traits
(4) keep farm crops free of all mutations

15 On hot, dry days, guard cells often close microscopic openings in plant leaves, conserving water. This is an example of

(1) environmental factors causing gene mutation in plants
(2) finite resources acting as selecting agents for evolution
(3) a feedback mechanism for maintaining homeostasis
(4) differentiation in plants as a result of stimuli

16 The diagram below represents a portion of a DNA molecule.

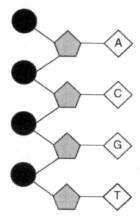

The letters represent different types of

(1) sugar molecules        (3) enzymes
(2) molecular bases        (4) proteins

17 Cotton plants produce seeds that contain high-quality protein. This protein could be used as a food source except that the seeds are poisonous to humans. Recently, scientists have inserted a section of DNA into the cotton plants that makes the cotton seeds nonpoisonous. The technique for this procedure is known as

(1) gene manipulation        (3) reproduction
(2) cloning        (4) direct harvesting

18 Which mutation in a fruit fly could be passed on to its offspring?

(1) a mutation in a cell of an eye that changes the color of the eye
(2) a mutation in a leg cell that causes the leg to be shorter
(3) a mutation in a sperm cell that changes the shape of the wing
(4) a mutation in a cell of the digestive tract that produces a different enzyme

19 Which process initially provides the link between an abiotic factor and the energy needs of an entire ecosystem?

(1) respiration                                   (3) decomposition
(2) photosynthesis                                (4) predation

20 Buffalo grass is a species of plant found on the grazing prairies of Wyoming. It is a tough grass that has silicates (compounds containing oxygen and silicon) that reinforce its leaves. For hundreds of years, this grass has survived in an adverse environment. Which statement best explains the presence of this grass today?

(1) There are no variations in this grass species that help it to survive in an adverse environment.
(2) Silicates are necessary for photosynthesis.
(3) The current species has no mutations.
(4) The silicates in the grass have given the species an advantage in its environment.

21 The bud shown in the diagram below was produced by asexual reproduction.

Bud

Which process is responsible for the formation of the bud?

(1) fertilization                                 (3) mitosis
(2) recombination                                 (4) meiosis

22 The temporary storage of energy in ATP molecules is part of which process?

(1) cell division                                 (3) protein synthesis
(2) cellular respiration                          (4) DNA replication

23 A function of white blood cells is to

(1) transport oxygen to body cells
(2) produce hormones that regulate cell communication
(3) carry glucose to body cells
(4) protect the body against pathogens

24 Competition for biotic resources can be illustrated by organisms fighting for a limited amount of

(1) air to breathe                    (3) mates for breeding
(2) water to drink                    (4) space for nesting

25 Many biological catalysts, hormones, and receptor molecules are similar in that, in order to function properly, they must

(1) interact with each other at a high pH
(2) interact with molecules that can alter their specific bonding patterns
(3) contain amino acid chains that fold into a specific shape
(4) contain identical DNA base sequences

26 If only one type of tree is planted in an abandoned field, the ecosystem will

(1) evolve quickly and become extinct
(2) be unable to reach dynamic equilibrium
(3) contain little genetic variability
(4) be unable to cycle materials

27 Which organisms directly help to reduce overpopulation in a deer herd?

(1) parasites and predators
(2) parasites and scavengers
(3) decomposers and predators
(4) decomposers and consumers

28 In the human body, oxygen is absorbed by the lungs and nutrients are absorbed by the small intestine. In a single-celled organism, this absorption directly involves the

(1) nucleus                           (3) cell membrane
(2) chloroplasts                      (4) chromosomes

29 An earthworm lives and reproduces in the soil. It aerates the soil and adds organic material to it. The earthworm is a source of food for other organisms. All of these statements together best describe

(1) a habitat
(2) autotrophic nutrition
(3) an ecological niche
(4) competition

30 Depletion of nonrenewable resources is often a result of

(1) environmental laws
(2) human population growth
(3) reforestation
(4) recycling

---

## Part B–1    Answer all questions in this part.  [13 points]

*Directions* (31–43): For *each* statement or question, write on the separate answer sheet the *number* of the word or expression that, of those given, best completes the statement or answers the question.

31 The bar graph below shows the height of a plant at the end of each week of a five-week growth period.

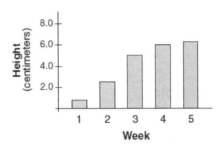

Which statement represents a valid conclusion based on the information in the graph?

(1) The plant was given water during the first three weeks, only.
(2) The plant will grow faster during the sixth week than it did during the fifth week.
(3) The plant grew fastest during the first three weeks, and then it grew slower.
(4) The plant grew slowest during the first three weeks, and then it grew faster.

32 A diagram frequently used in ecological studies is shown below.

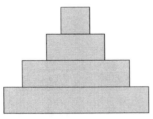

This diagram can be used to represent the

(1) dependency of animal survival on physical conditions in an ecosystem
(2) loss of energy from various groups of organisms in an ecosystem
(3) competition among species in an ecosystem
(4) mechanisms that maintain homeostasis in the plants in an ecosystem

33 A biologist formulates a hypothesis, performs experiments to test his hypothesis, makes careful observations, and keeps accurate records of his findings. In order to complete this process, the biologist should

(1) adjust the data to support the hypothesis
(2) eliminate data that do not support the hypothesis
(3) write a research paper explaining his theories before performing his experiments, in order to gain funding sources
(4) evaluate the findings and, if necessary, alter the hypothesis based on his findings, and test the new hypothesis

Base your answer to question 34 on the diagram below and on your knowledge of biology.

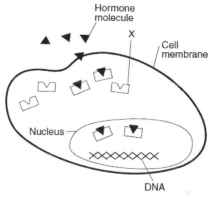

34 Structure $X$ most likely functions in the

(1) transport of chemical messenger molecules into the cell nucleus
(2) extraction of energy from nutrients
(3) separation of cell contents from the outside environment
(4) digestion of large molecules

35 The arrows in the diagram below represent the movement of materials.

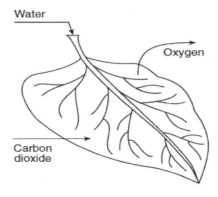

Water

Oxygen

Carbon
dioxide

This movement of materials indicated by the arrows is most directly involved in the processes of

(1) respiration and replication
(2) photosynthesis and excretion
(3) digestion and recycling
(4) circulation and coordination

36 When using a compound light microscope, the most common reason for staining a specimen being observed is to

(1) keep the organism from moving around
(2) make the view more colorful
(3) determine the effects of chemicals on the organism
(4) reveal details that are otherwise not easily seen

Base your answers to questions 37 through 39 on the diagram below and on your knowledge of biology.

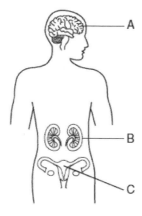

37 Failure of structure *A* to function properly would most directly disrupt

(1) autotrophic nutrition
(2) chromosome replication
(3) cellular communication
(4) biological evolution

38 Structure *B* represents

(1) cells, only
(2) cells and tissues, only
(3) an organ with cells and tissues
(4) a complete system with organs, tissues, and cells

39 Structure *C* is part of which body system?

(1) digestive            (3) circulatory
(2) reproductive        (4) nervous

40 Thrips are insects that feed on the pollen and flowers of certain plants. The size of a thrip population depends on the number of flowers available. Which graph best represents changes in a population of thrips if winter was longer than usual and the summer was too cool and dry for many flowers to bloom?

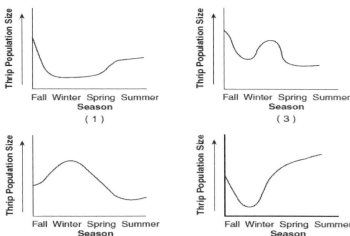

41 The percent of DNA that species *A* has in common with species *B*, *C*, *D*, and *E* are shown in the graph below.

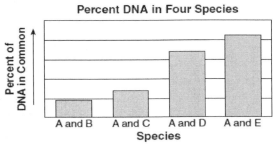

Which statement is a valid conclusion that can be drawn from this graph?

(1) Species *A* is closely related to species *B*, but is not related to species *E*.
(2) Fewer mutations have occurred in species *B* and *C* than in species *A*.
(3) Species *A* and *E* have the greatest similarity in protein structure.
(4) Environment influences the rate of evolution.

Base your answers to questions 42 and 43 on the passage below and on your knowledge of biology.

...Corals come in about 1,500 known species—from soft swaying fans to stony varieties with hard skeletons that form reef bases. They are made up of polyps, tiny animals that live in colonies and feed at night on microscopic plants and creatures. The coral's surface is the living part, with color infused by single-celled algae called zooxanthellae that live in polyp tissue. The algae act like solar panels, passing energy to the coral as they photosynthesize while feeding on the coral's waste. Extremely sensitive, corals survive in a narrow range of temperature, sunlight and salinity. An uncommonly severe El Niño in 1998 raised ocean temperatures and changed currents, causing bleaching that devastated reefs worldwide. Scientists say parts of the Indian Ocean lost up to 90 percent of corals. The bleaching struck reefs around the Persian Gulf, East Africa, Southeast Asia and the Caribbean. Some recovered. Many died. ...

42 The relationship between the polyps and the zooxanthellae can best be described as

(1) negative for both
(2) neutral for both
(3) positive for both
(4) negative for one and positive for the other

43 The passage contains information concerning

(1) limiting factors
(2) reproductive methods
(3) bacteria
(4) competition

**Day 29**

**Stop:** Check your answers and note how many correct **Points**

## Part A

| | | |
|---|---|---|
| 1) 3 | 11) 2 | 21) 3 |
| 2) 2 | 12) 2 | 22) 2 |
| 3) 4 | 13) 1 | 23) 4 |
| 4) 2 | 14) 3 | 24) 3 |
| 5) 3 | 15) 3 | 25) 3 |
| 6) 2 | 16) 2 | 26) 3 |
| 7) 3 | 17) 1 | 27) 1 |
| 8) 3 | 18) 3 | 28) 3 |
| 9) 1 | 19) 2 | 29) 3 |
| 10) 4 | 20) 4 | 30) 2 |

## Part B-1

| | |
|---|---|
| 31) 3 | 39) 2 |
| 32) 2 | 40) 1 |
| 33) 4 | 41) 3 |
| 34) 1 | 42) 3 |
| 35) 2 | 43) 1 |
| 36) 4 | |
| 37) 3 | |
| 38) 3 | |

Start: Answer all questions in B-2, C and D before stopping.

**Part B–2:** Answer all questions in this part. (12 point)

*Directions* (44–55): For those questions that are followed by four choices, circle the *number* preceding the choice that, of those given, best completes the statement or answers the question. For all other questions in

44 State *one* way insect pests in an apple orchard can be controlled without using chemical pesticides. [1]

_____

_____

45 The tranquilizer thalidomide was once prescribed for pregnant women. When this drug was used between the third and sixth week after fertilization, serious deformities in the fetus occurred as the fetus developed. State why thalidomide would have a greater effect on development when used between weeks 3 and 6 than when used in late pregnancy. [1]

_____

_____

_____

46 Draw an arrow to indicate *one* part of the plant cell below that would *not* be found in an animal cell. The tip of the arrow must touch the part being identified. [1]

Base your answers to questions 47 and 48 on the information and chart below and on your knowledge of biology.

Body weight is considered to be a risk factor for diseases such as diabetes and high blood pressure. The Body Mass Index (BMI) chart can be used as a guide to determine if a person's body weight puts them at risk for such diseases. A portion of this chart is shown below.

### Calculating Your Body Mass Index (BMI)

| | Healthy | | Overweight | | | | | Obese | | | |
|---|---|---|---|---|---|---|---|---|---|---|---|
| BMI | 19 | 24 | 25 | 26 | 27 | 28 | 29 | 30 | 35 | 40 | 45 |
| Height | Weight in Pounds | | | | | | | | | | |
| 5'4" | 110 | 140 | 145 | 151 | 157 | 163 | 169 | 174 | 204 | 232 | 262 |
| 5'5" | 114 | 144 | 150 | 156 | 162 | 168 | 174 | 180 | 210 | 240 | 270 |
| 5'6" | 118 | 148 | 155 | 161 | 167 | 173 | 179 | 186 | 216 | 247 | 278 |
| 5'7" | 121 | 153 | 159 | 166 | 172 | 178 | 185 | 191 | 223 | 255 | 287 |
| 5'8" | 125 | 158 | 164 | 171 | 177 | 184 | 190 | 197 | 230 | 262 | 295 |
| 5'9" | 128 | 162 | 169 | 176 | 182 | 189 | 196 | 203 | 236 | 270 | 304 |
| 5'10" | 132 | 167 | 174 | 181 | 188 | 195 | 202 | 209 | 243 | 278 | 313 |
| 5'11" | 136 | 172 | 179 | 186 | 193 | 200 | 208 | 215 | 250 | 286 | 322 |

47 The BMI for a person who is 5 feet 9 inches tall and weighs 170 pounds is between

(1) 24 and 25                 (3) 27 and 28
(2) 25 and 26                 (4) 29 and 30

48 Is the person described in question 47 at risk for diseases such as diabetes or high blood pressure? Support your answer. [1]

_____

_____

49 The diagram below represents a food web.

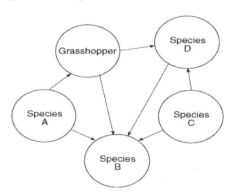

Which species would most likely be a decomposer?

(1) *A*                                          (3) *C*
(2) *B*                                          (4) *D*

***Base your answers to questions 50 and 51 on the passage below and on your knowledge of biology.***

Plants of the snow lotus species, *Saussurea laniceps*, are used in Tibet and China to produce traditional medicines. These plants bloom just once, at the end of a seven-year life span. Collectors remove the taller blooming plants, which they consider to have the best medicinal value. Some scientists are concerned that the continual selection and removal of the tall plants from natural ecosystems may result in a change in the average height of the snow lotus in future populations.

50 The removal of the taller plants is an example of

(1) genetic engineering                      (3) selective breeding
(2) direct harvesting                        (4) asexual reproduction

51 State *one* way that the removal of the taller snow lotus plants from ecosystems interferes with the process of natural selection. [1]

_____

_____

_____

_____

*Base your answers to questions 52 through 55 on the information below and on your knowledge of biology.*

    A biology class conducted an experiment to determine the rate of respiration of yeast in bread dough at various temperatures.

    Bread dough will rise due to the production of carbon dioxide by the yeast present in the dough.

    An equal amount of dough was placed in the bottom of each of five graduated cylinders. Each cylinder was then placed in a different water bath to maintain a particular temperature. A diagram of the setup is shown below.

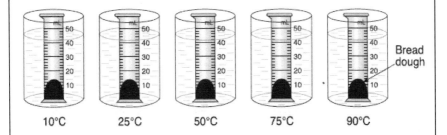

  10°C          25°C          50°C          75°C          90°C

The amount of expansion of the dough in each cylinder was measured after 15 minutes. The results are shown in the data table below.

### The Effect of Temperature on Yeast Respiration

| Temperature of Water Bath (°C) | Change in Volume of Bread Dough (mL) |
|:---:|:---:|
| 10 | 4 |
| 25 | 11 |
| 50 | 20 |
| 75 | 25 |
| 90 | 2 |

*Directions (52–53): Using the information in the data table, construct a line graph on the grid, following the directions below.*

52 Mark an appropriate scale, without any breaks, on the axis labeled "Temperature of Water Bath (°C)." [1]

53 Plot the data from the data table. Surround each point with a small circle and connect the points. [1]

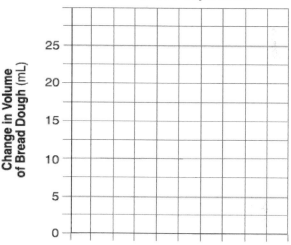

**The Effect of Temperature on Yeast Respiration**

54 At which temperature did yeast cells produce the *least* amount of gas in 15 minutes? [1]

_____ °C

55 Identify the independent variable in this investigation. [1]

_____

## Part C    Answer all questions in this part. [17 Points]

*Directions* (56–67): Record your answers in the spaces provided in this examination booklet.

*Base your answer to question 56–59 on the information below and on your knowledge of biology.*

> Many people have a sensitivity to peanuts. The symptoms can include watery, itchy eyes and difficulty breathing. This allergic reaction can be mild, severe, or fatal.

56–59 Discuss why an individual can have a sensitivity to peanuts. In your answer, be sure to:

- identify the human system that is responsible for this sensitivity to peanuts [1]
- identify the specific type of molecule that triggers an allergic reaction [1]
- state *one* reason why a person could be allergic to peanuts, but *not* be allergic to walnuts [1]
- describe how this reaction is similar to the rejection of a transplanted organ [1]

_____

_____

_____

_____

_____

_____

60 State *one* way the decision of high school students to drive to school rather than ride a bus to school can
have a *negative* environmental impact on future generations. [1]

_____

_____

*Base your answers to questions 61 through 64 on the passage below and on your knowledge of biology.*

Dandelions are weeds that are very common in many grassy areas of New York State. Dandelion flowers first open up in a bright-yellow stage, and later turn a fluffy white when they are ready to release their seeds. The seeds are carried by the wind, and can sometimes travel great distances before landing and growing into new plants. The stems of dandelions are usually very long, typically about 20–30 centimeters (cm), and stand high above the surrounding grass.

A science teacher in Niagara County discovered an area in her lawn where nearly every dandelion had a stem less than 1 cm long. These short dandelions were replacing large amounts of grass in the lawn surrounding her house. They were growing much more thickly than the taller dandelions in other nearby areas. The short dandelions appeared to be growing very successfully in one area of her lawn, but did not appear to have spread to other areas of her lawn. The science teacher noticed that every time she mowed her lawn, the short dandelions were left untouched by the mower blades, and that their numbers were steadily increasing.

61 State *one* possible cause of the genetic variation in dandelion height. [1]

_____

62 State *one* possible explanation for the fact that the short dandelions had not yet spread to other areas of her lawn. [1]

_____

_____

63 State *one* possible reason why the amount of grass was decreasing, while the number of short dandelions was increasing in the lawn of the science teacher. [1]

_____

_____

64 State *one* possible advantage the short dandelions may have over the tall dandelions in this yard. [1]

_____

_____

*Base your answers to questions 65 and 66 on the information below and on your knowledge of biology.*

The New York State Department of Health issues health advisories on eating specific fish. Some of these fish contain toxic chemicals that were passed through the food chain and accumulate in the tissues of these fish. The advisories include general advice on fish caught in specific bodies of water. The advisory tells people how to minimize their exposure to toxins in these fish in order to reduce health risks associated with them.

65 Different species of fish are found in different positions in a food chain, depending on what they eat.
Explain how the position of a fish in a food chain would affect the amount of toxins present in the tissues of the fish. [1]

_____

_____


66 State *one* action that could be taken to reduce the amount of toxins present in the environment inhabited by these fish. [1]

_____

_____

*Base your answers to questions 67 and 68 on the information below and on your knowledge of biology.*

The diagram below represents some stages in the life cycle of humans. The numbers in the diagram represent various processes in the cycle.

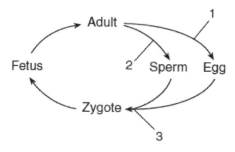

67 State how processes 1 and 2 affect the amount of genetic information provided by a parent to its offspring. [1]

_____

_____

68 State how process 3 affects the amount of genetic information an offspring receives. [1]

_____

_____

69 Suggest *one* way that doctors or patients can help to reduce the chances of bacteria becoming resistant to an antibiotic. [1]

_____

_____

*Base your answers to questions 70 through 72 on the information below and on your knowledge of biology.*

In the 1980s, global deforestation was estimated at 17 to 20 million hectares per year, an area the size of Great Britain. Today, the area affected by deforestation has decreased significantly in some regions of the world through the use of sustainable forest management. However, there are still regions of the world affected by wide-scale deforestation, because of the short-term economic benefits. The harmful effects of deforestation on regional and worldwide climate and ecology continue as forest areas are destroyed.

70 State *one* short-term economic benefit of deforestation. [1]

_____

_____

71 Explain how deforestation decreases biodiversity. [1]

_____

_____

72 Explain how wide-scale deforestation may contribute to global warming. [1]

_____

_____

## Part D:    Answer all questions in this part. [13 points]

*Directions* (73–85): For those questions that are multiple choice, record on your separate answer sheet the *number* of the choice that best completes the statement or answers the question. For all other questions in this part, follow directions given in the question and record your answer in the spaces provided.

73 A model cell setup is represented in the "Initial State" diagram below.

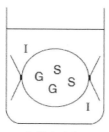

| Key |
|-----|
| S = starch |
| G = glucose |
| I = starch indicator |

Initial state

Which diagram indicates the areas where each of these substances would be located after 20 minutes? [1]

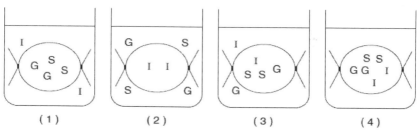

( 1 )          ( 2 )          ( 3 )          ( 4 )

74 Which factor most likely contributed to the evolution of Galapagos Islands finches with different beak shapes?

(1) similar climates on the different islands
(2) competition between the finches for food
(3) cloning experiments carried out by native people on the islands
(4) increased rate of asexual reproduction

*Base your answer to question 75 on the finch diversity diagram below and on your knowledge of biology.*

## Variations in Beaks of Galapagos Islands Finches

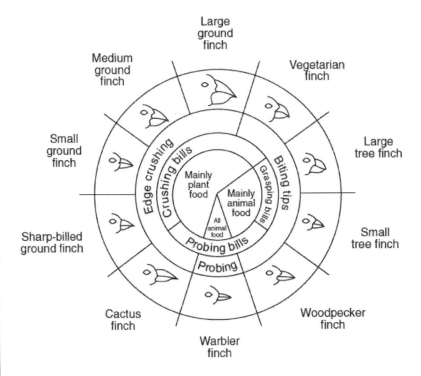

From: *Galapagos: A Natural History Guide*

75 Warbler finches are classified as

(1) producers

(2) herbivores

(3) carnivores

(4) decomposers

Base your answers to questions 76 through 78 on the diagram below and on your knowledge of biology.

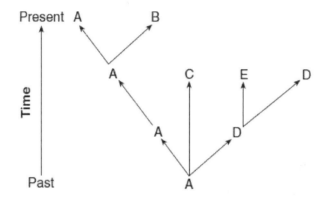

Letters *A* through *E* represent different species of organisms. The arrows represent long periods of geologic time.

76 Which species would most likely show the greatest similarities in their amino acid sequences?

(1) *A* and *E*            (3) *B* and *D*
(2) *A* and *B*            (4) *C* and *E*

77 Which species is the common ancestor to all of the other species? [1]

_____

78 Identify *one* species that was *not* able to adapt to its environment. Support your answer. [1]

_____

_____

_____

    

Base your answers to questions 79 through 81 on the information and diagram below and on your knowledge of biology. The diagram represents some of the steps in a procedure used in a specific laboratory activity.

Samples of DNA from an eye-color gene of four individuals, *W, X, Y,* and *Z,* were cut into pieces using a type of chemical. The results of this procedure are shown below.

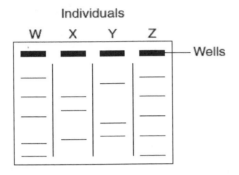

Individuals

79 Identify the specific type of chemical used to cut the DNA in this procedure. [1]

_____

80 Which *two* individuals have DNA base patterns for this gene that are the most similar? Support your answer. [1]

Individuals: _____ and _____

_____

_____

81 The diagram represents the results of the procedure known as

(1) cloning                              (3) gel electrophoresis
(2) chromatography                       (4) protein sequencing

Base your answer to question 82 on the results of an experiment using plant pigments represented below and on your knowledge of biology.

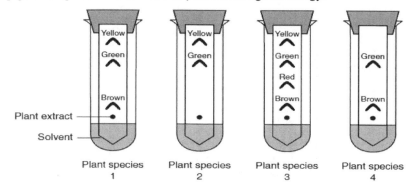

82 Which phrase could be used to describe this technique?

(1) the use of chromatography to separate molecules in a mixture
(2) the use of cut leaves to observe certain colors
(3) using indicators to determine pH
(4) using dichotomous keys to identify plants

Base your answers to questions 83 and 84 on the information below and on your knowledge of biology.

    A student checked her pulse rate three times during one day. When she first woke up, her pulse rate was 54 beats per minute (bpm). As she walked to her first-period class, it was 71 bpm. Later, she recorded 98 bpm after playing in a basketball game.

83 State *one* reason for the change in her pulse rate throughout the day. [1]

_____

_____

84 State *one* way a change in pulse rate helps to meet the needs of the body. [1]

_____

_____

85 The diagram below shows a student heating some test tubes with chemicals in them during a laboratory activity.

Explain why putting stoppers in the test tubes could be dangerous. [1]

_____

_____

**Day 30**

Stop: Correct your answers and note how many correct **Points**

## Part B-2

**44. 1 point**      **Acceptable responses include, but are not limited to:**

*Increase the number of natural predators of the insect pest*

*Use a biological control*

*Use flypaper/traps*

**45. 1 point**      **Acceptable responses include, but are not limited to:**

*Most organs begin to develop between weeks 3 and 6, whereas, in late pregnancy, these organs are fully formed.*

*In late pregnancy, major organs would already have been formed and less damage would have occurred.*

**46. 1 point**      For indicating *one* of the three correct plant parts, shown below.

**Examples of 1-credit responses for question 46:**

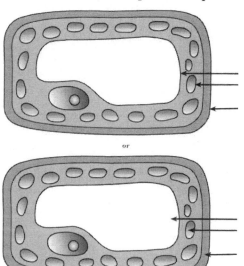

*or*

47. **1 point**   *2*

48. **1 point**   **Acceptable responses include, but are not limited to:**

*The BMI indicates the person is overweight and is therefore at risk for these diseases.*

*There is a slight risk because the BMI places the person in the overweight range, but not in the obese range.*

*yes, because the BMI is over 25*

49. **1 point**   *2*

50. **1 point**   *2*

51. **1 point**   **Acceptable responses include, but are not limited to:**

*It results in a smaller gene pool.*

*It reduces the variety available for selection within populations.*

*Tall varieties would not have a chance to reproduce.*

*Removes genes for tallness from the population*

**52. 1 point**     *For marking an appropriate scale, without any breaks, on the "Temperature of Water Bath (°C)" axis.*

**53. 1 point**     *For correctly plotting the data and connecting the points.*

**Example of a 2-credit graph for questions 52 and 53**

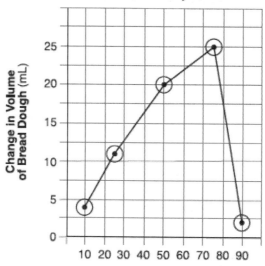

**The Effect of Temperature
on Yeast Respiration**

*Change in Volume of Bread Dough (mL)* (y-axis)

*Temperature of Water Bath (°C)* (x-axis)

**54. 1 point**     ***90°C***     or     *for temperature that is consistent with the student's graph for questions 52 and 53.*

**55. 1 point**     *Temperature.*

56. 1 point    **Acceptable response includes:**

*Any human system (nervous, respiratory, excretory..etc)*
***except circulatory***

57. 1 point    **Acceptable responses include, but are not limited to:**
*Antigen*
*Protein*
*Allergen*

58. 1 point    **Acceptable responses include, but are not limited to:**
*One type of antibody only reacts with (fits) one type of antigen.*
*Antibody reactions are specific.*
*Walnuts and peanuts have different proteins.*
*Walnuts and peanuts are made up of different chemicals.*

59. 1 point    **Acceptable responses include, but are not limited to:**
*Transplanted organs also have antigens that will stimulate antibodies that will attack the organ.*
*They both stimulate immune responses.*

60. 1 point    **Acceptable responses include, but are not limited to:**
*Global warming is impacted when more carbon dioxide is produced by many cars driven by the same number of students that could be transported by a few buses.*
*The exhaust from additional cars may lead to air pollution that will affect the environment for years.*

61. 1 point    **Acceptable responses include, but are not limited to:**
*mutation*
*Changes in DNA*
*Recombination/recombining of genes*

**62. 1 point**      **Acceptable responses include, but are not limited to:**

*The seeds from plants with shorter stems are less likely to be carried by the wind.*

*The short dandelions do not have an adaptation needed for survival in other areas of the lawn.*

*The seeds from the shorter dandelions did not land there.*

**63. 1 point**      **Acceptable responses include, but are not limited to:**

*The dandelions out-compete the grass for the same limited resources.*

*The dandelions are better adapted for survival.*

*The dandelions shade the grass.*

**64. 1 point**      **Acceptable responses include, but are not limited to:**

*Short dandelions are less likely to be cut down by a lawnmower.*

*Short dandelions will be left to reproduce.*

**65. 1 point**      **Acceptable responses include, but are not limited to:**

*Organisms higher up in the food chain have a high concentration of toxins because they eat more of the organisms lower in the food chain and build up the concentration in their tissue.*

*Predators have a high concentration because they eat organisms that have already accumulated toxins.*

**66. 1 point**      **Acceptable responses include, but are not limited to:**

*Pass laws to force individuals/companies to stop polluting.*

*Reduce runoff of environmental hazards from farms, roadways, or parking lots.*

*Remove the toxins from the environment.*

*Develop nontoxic alternatives to these chemicals.*

    

67. **1 point**   **Acceptable responses include, but are not limited to:**

*These processes reduce the amount of genetic information from each parent by half.*

*Each parent only contributes half of the genetic information that is contained in his or her own cells.*

*Each egg (or each sperm) will carry only half of the genetic information contained in the parent's body cells.*

68. **1 point**   **Acceptable responses include, but are not limited to:**

*This process ensures that offspring will have all the genetic information needed.*

*Fertilization restores the full number of chromosomes characteristic of the species.*

*When the sperm and egg combine, the zygote will contain a full set of chromosomes.*

69. **1 point**   **Acceptable responses include, but are not limited to:**

*Doctors should prescribe antibiotics only for bacterial infections.*

*Patients should not use antibiotics without the advice of a doctor.*

*Patients should use the antibiotic for the prescribed number of days, and not stop taking it when they feel better.*

*Do not use antibiotics for viral infections.*

70. **1 point**   **Acceptable responses include, but are not limited to:**

*Obtain more farmland*

*More lumber available for sale*

*Decrease the cost of lumber*

*Space to build larger communities*

*Increased profit*

*More jobs available*

71. **1 point**     **Acceptable responses include, but are not limited to:**

*Organisms lose habitats*

*Many different species are removed*

*Some species may become extinct*

72. **1 point**     **Acceptable responses include, but are not limited to:**

*With fewer plants to absorb carbon dioxide, the carbon dioxide remains in the atmosphere, contributing to the greenhouse effect that causes global warming.*

*If the trees are burned, carbon dioxide will be added to the atmosphere.*

## Part D

73. **1 point**     *3*

74. **1 point**     *2*

75. **1 point**     *3*

76. **1 point**     *2*

77. **1 point**     *A*

78. **1 point**     *For Choosing Species C, D or E and for supporting your answer*

**Acceptable responses include, but are not limited to:**
*Species C, because it became extinct.*
*D, because it is no longer alive.*
*Species E does not continue to the present.*

79. **1 point**     **Acceptable responses include, but are not limited to:**
*Enzymes*
*Restriction enzymes*
*Biological catalyst*

80. **1 point**     *For Choosing W and Z and for supporting your answer*

**Acceptable responses include, but are not limited to:**
*Because 4 of the 5 bands are identical*
*They have the greatest number of matching bands.*

81. **1 point**     3

82. **1 point**     1

83. **1 point**    **Acceptable responses include, but are not limited to:**

*When the student was sleeping, her activity was minimal and her pulse rate was slow. When she was walking, she used more energy, resulting in an increased pulse rate.*

*Pulse rate varies with activity level.*

*Her body was maintaining homeostasis.*

*Her heart beats faster when she is more active.*

84. **1 point**    **Acceptable responses include, but are not limited to:**

*Increased pulse rate increases the availability of food and oxygen to cells.*

*The pulse rate is an indication of the activity level of the body. Additional food and oxygen is provided to body cells with an increase in pulse rate.*

*Increases the removal of wastes from cells*

85. **1 point**    **Acceptable responses include, but are not limited to:**

*The stoppers would pop out of the heated tubes and possibly injure someone.*

*The test tubes may explode.*

## 1. Your Raw Score: _____

Add your day 29 and day 30 points.

## 2. Your Regents Grade: _____

Use the conversion chart below. The Scale Score corresponding to your Raw Score is your Regents Grade for this exam.

| Raw Score | Scale Score | Raw Score | Scale Score | Raw Score | Scale Score |
|---|---|---|---|---|---|
| 85 | 100 | 56 | 78 | 27 | 49 |
| 84 | 98 | 55 | 77 | 26 | 48 |
| 83 | 97 | 54 | 76 | 25 | 46 |
| 82 | 97 | 53 | 76 | 24 | 45 |
| 81 | 96 | 52 | 75 | 23 | 44 |
| 80 | 95 | 51 | 74 | 22 | 42 |
| 79 | 94 | 50 | 73 | 21 | 41 |
| 78 | 94 | 49 | 73 | 20 | 39 |
| 77 | 93 | 48 | 72 | 19 | 37 |
| 76 | 92 | 47 | 71 | 18 | 36 |
| 75 | 91 | 46 | 70 | 17 | 34 |
| 74 | 91 | 45 | 69 | 16 | 33 |
| . 73 | 90 | 44 | 68 | 15 | 31 |
| 72 | 89 | 43 | 67 | 14 | 29 |
| 71 | 88 | 42 | 66 | 13 | 27 |
| 70 | 88 | 41 | 66 | 12 | 25 |
| 69 | 87 | 40 | 65 | 11 | 24 |
| 68 | 86 | 39 | 64 | 10 | 22 |
| 67 | 86 | 38 | 62 | 9 | 20 |
| 66 | 85 | 37 | 61 | 8 | 18 |
| 65 | 84 | 36 | 60 | 7 | 16 |
| 64 | 83 | 35 | 59 | 6 | 14 |
| 63 | 83 | 34 | 58 | 5 | 11 |
| 62 | 82 | 33 | 57 | 4 | 9 |
| 61 | 81 | 32 | 56 | 3 | 7 |
| 60 | 81 | 31 | 54 | 2 | 5 |
| 59 | 80 | 30 | 53 | 1 | 2 |
| 58 | 79 | 29 | 52 | 0 | 0 |
| 57 | 79 | 28 | 51 | | |

# Track Your Progress
## on
## Multiple Choice Questions

How well have you been improving on the multiple choice questions? It's easy to find out.

**Get the correct points** that you noted at the end of each multiple choice set on the days labeled on the x-axis of the graphs below.

**Plot the points** and connect the dots on the graphs below. You hope to see an upward trend on each graph.

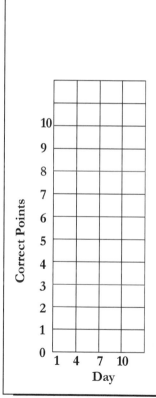

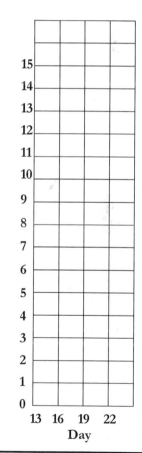

# Track Your Progress

## on
## Questions with Graphs, Tables and Diagrams

How well have you been improving on the multiple choice questions with graphs, tables and diagrams?   It's easy to find out.

**Get the correct points** that you noted at the end of each multiple choice set on the days labeled on the x-axis of the graphs below.

**Plot the points** and connect the dots on the graphs below. You hope to see an upward trend on each graph.

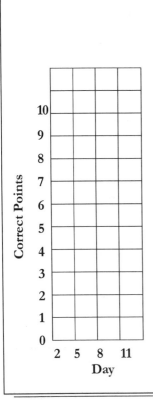

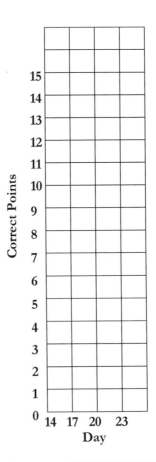

# Track Your Progress
## on
## Short Answer Questions

How well have you been improving on the short answer questions? It's easy to find out.

**Get the correct points** that you noted at the end of each short answer question sets on the days labeled on the x-axis of the graph below.

**Plot the points** and connect the dots on the graphs below. You hope to see an upward trend on each graph.

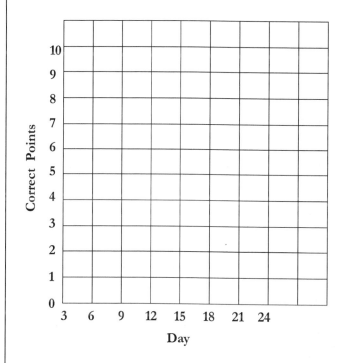

# Glossary

## A

**abiotic**
any nonliving conditions in an organism's environment (rock, pH, sunlight, temperature) that affect survival

**absorption**
the process by which materials such nutrients, water, gases, etc.. cross the cell membrane and are taken inside the cell

**acid rain**
rain that has a low (acidic) pH that is harmful to the environment - caused by pollution

**active transport** movement of materials across a cell membrane from an area of low concentration to an area of high concentration; requires energy

**adaptation**
organisms adjust to the changing environment by developing characteristics that are necessary for evolution

**AIDS**
a disease resulting from getting the HIV (a virus) which destroys ones immune system

**algae**
photosynthetic aquatic organisms; resembles a plant

**amino acids**
the building blocks of proteins; filtered through kidneys, excess is excreted in urine

**antibiotic**
a chemical that is usually injected that kills specific pathogens (penicillin, amoxicillin)

**antibodies**
molecules that organisms produce to defend against pathogens; attach to specific

**antigen**
a protein located on a pathogen that stimulates body to produce antibodies

**asexual reproduction**
involves one parent; no variation; body cells

**ATP**
a substance produced by organisms to be used as energy

## B

**bacteria**
a parasitic single-celled organism that can cause disease

**biodiversity**
the number of different species in an ecosystem; the higher it is, the healthier the ecosystem is

**biome**
a large area containing a specific climate with plants and animals

**biotechnology**
any procedure that involves new inventions or techniques to further science (cloning, selective breeding, gene splicing, stem cell replacement)

**biotic**
living parts in an organism's environment (predators, prey, plants)

**body cells**
cells that undergo asexual reproduction with a specific outcome (skin cells, tissue cells)

# C

**cancer**
a group of harmful cells (tumor) that invades healthy cells; able to be spread through blood stream

**carbohydrate**
an organic compound obtained from grains; example of monosaccharide is glucose, example of polysaccharide is starch

**carbon dioxide**
waste molecule excreted by animals and taken in by plants

**carcinogen**
a chemical which increases the risk of getting cancer (smoking and nicotine)

**carnivore**
an organism feeding on meat

**carrying capacity**
the maximum number of species in a population that an ecosystem can sustain

**cell membrane**
a boundary on every cell that is selectively permeable and regulates what substances enter and exits

**characteristics**
genetic traits of an organism

**chloroplasts**
an organelle only in plant cells; contains chlorophyll; carries out photosynthesis

**chromosomes**
structures in nucleus that contain genetic information circulation a life function; for animals: the movement of blood - main organ is the heart

**clone**
creating a new, genetically identical, organism from one cell of another organism

**competition**
occurs when organisms struggle for the same resources such as food, water, and living space.

**consumers**
an organism that obtains its energy from other organisms (most animals)

**consumption**
to obtain nutrients; for animals: to eat or drink

**coordination**
a life function; for animals: organizing muscles, bones, nerves, and receptors in order to maintain homeostasis

**culture**
a colony of microorganisms grown in nutrient (bacteria are often cultured in Petri dishes)

**cyclic**
changes repeated occurrences (day and night, moon phases)

**cytoplasm**
the fluid inside every cell cushioning organelles

## D

**decomposers**
an organism that obtains its food from dead organisms (many bacteria)

**deforestation**
the destruction of forests (logging)

**degrade**
to lesson or reduce the amount of something (deforestation degrades the forests)

**dependent**
a factor that must exist or remain common (dependent variable in an experiment)

**depletion**
take away or lessen the amount of something (rainforest depletion)

**detection**
becoming aware of something (early detection of cancer is important for successful treatment)

**development**
changes that occur in an organism starting with fertilization and ending with death

**diagnose**
identify a disease

**differentiation**
changes that cells undergo when they begin to multiply into their specific function

**diffusion**
the movement of materials across a cell membrane from an area of high concentration to an area of low concentration; does not require energy

**digestion**
a life function; breaking down food molecules before they can be absorbed into cells

**dissipate**
to disappear or go away

**diversity**
variation in characteristics or traits

**DNA (deoxyribonucleic acid)**
the hereditary material of all living organisms; the instruction for all characteristics and functions; made up of subunits

## E

**ecology**
the study of how living and nonliving things interact in an environment

**ecological**
community a group of different species or populations existing in the same area

**ecological succession**
the slow, natural, change from bedrock to a climax (maximum) forest

ecosystems
an area that has biotic and abiotic parts that are interacting

**egg**
the female reproductive gamete produced in the ovaries

**embryo**
beginning stages of development following the formation of a zygote

**embryonic development**
events that occur in developing from a zygote into a functional organism

**encoded**
(in genes) the location for a specific message for a specific trait/characteristic

**energy**
obtained through cellular respiration; often referred to as ATP

**energy pyramid**
a way of describing the flow of energy (consumers on top, producers on bottom)

**energy source**
where an organism gets its energy from; ultimate source is the Sun

**engineer**
plan or create something (as in genetic engineering)

**environment(al)**
everything included in your surroundings

**enzyme**
a protein that is necessary for all chemical reactions to occur

**equilibrium**
steady-state; to be equal

**estrogen**
major female steroid hormone (a protein); involved with pregnancy and works with
progesterone

**evolution**
a gradual process where organisms change into more complex forms; organisms
(species) adapt in order to survive

**excretion**
remove metabolic wastes; in animals: may be urine, sweat, or exhalation

**expression**
a trait or characteristic that is visible or shown  extinction the death of every
individual of a particular species

**F**

**fats organic**
compound providing long-term energy storage; made up of glycerol and fatty acids

**feedback mechanism**
when there is a change in the environment, an organisms is stimulated to produce a
change in itself in order to maintain homeostasis

**fertilization**
the joining of sperm cell and egg cell to form a zygote

**fetus**
a developing embryo; cells undergoing differentiation

**food chain**
a way of describing the transfer of energy from one organism to another (one-way

**food web**
a way of describing the transfer of energy from one organism to another

**fossil fuels**
nonrenewable forms of energy that came from the remains of organisms (coal, natural gas, oil)

**fossils**
remains of dead organisms preserved by natural occurrences (evidence of evolution)

**fungi**
plant-like organism that lack chlorophyll (yeast, mold, mushrooms); may act as a pathogen

**G**

**gametes**
sex cells with one-half as many chromosomes as normal cell that combine to form a zygote during fertilization (sperm or egg)

**gene**
segment of chromosome that has the genetic information for a trait (the human genome project has identified every gene in the human)

**gene expression**
traits or characteristics that are made known

**gene mutation**
an error in the DNA code, thus changing a specific trait or characteristic (sickle-cell anemia, cystic fibrosis)

**genetic engineering**
to manipulate genes; similar to biotechnology and recombinant gene technology

**genetic variation**
the differences in offspring that are passed from generation to generation

**geologic time**
categorizing or separating the past through major geologic processes

**global**
warming an atmospheric increase in average temperature of the Earth due to an excess of carbon dioxide

**glucose**
simple carbohydrate necessary for the production of ATP; also represented as $C_6H_{12}O_6$

**guard cells**
located on plants which regulate the intake and excretion of water and gases in order to maintain homeostasis

# H

**habitat**
where an organism lives

**herbivore**
organism feeding only of plants (deer, cow)

**heredity**
the genetic passing down of DNA from parent to daughter

**homeostasis**
maintaining a constant internal environment

**hormones**
chemical substances (proteins) that are secreted from glands to maintain homeostasis

**host**
an organism that houses a parasite  human impact the affects of what humans have on the environment

# I

**imbalance**
a lack of even distribution; a disruption in homeostasis

**immune system**
a life function involved with protecting against infection

**industrialization**
sudden development or massive construction - usually the cause of pollution

**infection**
the invasion by a pathogen into an organism - usually causes harm

**inherit**
to receive particular genetic traits form parents during fertilization

**inorganic**
any chemical or compound that does not contain carbon

**insulin**
secreted by the pancreas to ensure blood sugar levels are at homeostasis (diabetics do not naturally produce insulin, it must be injected)

**interaction**
when two or more organisms are occupying the same habitat

**interdependence**
when one organism is dependent upon another organism for survival

**internal environment**
inside every cell in every organism (usually is used in relation with homeostasis)

# K

**karyotype**
a picture of the full set of chromosomes arranged by size and shape

# L

**life functions**
those activities working together in order to survive (respiration, excretion, locomotion, transport, regulation, digestion, regulation)

**limiting factor**
something in an organisms' environment that determines its survival (predators, sunlight, pH, water)

# M

**manipulate**
to manually change something; usually refers to working with biotechnology

**meiosis**
a way that cells replicate (usually describing the formation of gametes); the division of one cell into four cells, each with one-half as many chromosomes as the original cell; daughter cells have variation

**metabolism**
all of the life functions/processes/activities working together to build and break down chemical reactions

**microbes**
a very small life form (microorganisms)

**mitochondria**
cell organelle involved with the production of energy (ATP); there are many of these per animal cell

**mitosis**
a way that cells replicate (usually describing the formation of body cells or microorganism reproduction); the division of one cell into two identical cells

**multicellular**
containing more than one cell; usually referring to organisms other than protists

**mutation**
an error in the DNA code, thus changing a specific trait or characteristic (sickle-cell anemia, cystic fibrosis)

# N

**natural disaster**
a natural occurring event which usually disrupts the ecology

**natural selection**
those species that have the most adaptive traits for an environment are more likely to survive and reproduce

**niche**
an organism's job or role in its ecosystem; when two niches overlap, there may be competition for resources

**nucleus**
cell organelle containing the genetic material (only one of these in each cell)

# O

**organ**
a group of organized specialized tissues that perform certain life function

**organ system**
a group of organs that work together to complete a specific task (esophagus, stomach, small and large intestines are organs which make up the digestive system)

**organelles**
different structures within each cell that perform specific tasks (mitochondria, vacuole, nucleus)

**organic**
compounds that contain, among others, carbon - all living things organisms a living thing that performs all life functions

**ovaries**
female reproductive unit that produces and releases eggs (normal women have two ovaries)

**oxygen**
waste molecule excreted by plants and inhaled by animals

**ozone**
depletion reducing the amount of ozone ($O_3$) in the ozone layer

**ozone layer**
part of the atmosphere that blocks harmful ultraviolet rays from reaching the Earths surface

# P

**parasite**
an organism that lives on and is dependent on its host - harm is done to the host

**pathogens**
any organism that causes harm to another (virus, bacteria)

**pesticides**
harmful chemicals added to plants to kill insects that are destroying the plants

**pH**
a measure of something to determine if it is more acidic or basic. Measured from a scale of 1-7 . Most acidic = 1,   neutral  = 7,  most basic = 7

**photosynthesis**
a process occurring in plants  (Light energy + $H_2O$  +   $CO_2$ ---- > $C_6H_{12}O_6$  + $O_2$ )

**physiology**
the study of how an organism's body functions together

**pollution**
making unclean; contamination

**population**
in reference to ecology, a group of the same species living together

**population growth**
a way of looking at how quickly a population is increasing or decreasing - if increasing, will eventually reach its carrying capacity

**predator**
an organism that feeds on prey

**prey**
an organism that is eaten by predators

**producer**
organisms that makes its own food (plants); opposite to consumers

**progesterone**
female steroid hormone involved with pregnancy; works with estrogen

**protein**
organic compound made up of amino acids (hormones, enzymes, antibodies)

# R

**radiation**
rays that are emitted which are harmful to organisms as in radioactivity

**raw materials**
the most basic building blocks for a system; unused materials

**receptor**
microscopic structures that receive specific messages thus allowing a reaction to occur (as in: nerves, enzymes, antibodies)

**recombination**
usually refers to combining two or more different pieces of DNA into one DNA molecule

**recycle**
to reuse waste; a positive human impact on our environment

**regulation**
to control all other life functions

**replicate**
duplicating DNA during cell division (mitosis and meiosis)

**reproductive**
technology using present scientific techniques to produce offspring (in vitro fertilization, cloning)

**respiration**
a life function where gas exchange occurs

**response**
an organism's reaction to an internal or external stimuli

**ribosome**
cell organelle where the synthesis (formation) of proteins occur

**risks**
behaviors which are harmful to others (smoking, taking drugs during pregnancy)

**RNA (ribonucleic acid)**
contains base sequences codes necessary for protein synthesis

**r-RNA (ribosomal RNA)**
RNA that makes up the ribosome

**scavenger**
an organism that feeds on dead organisms

**selective breeding**
an example of biotechnology where humans pick and choose the result

**sequence**
the arrangement of subunits in a DNA code

**sex cells (gametes)**
monoploid cells (sperm and eggs) each containing half an organism genetic materials

**sexual reproduction**
usually requires a male and female parent; there is variation in genetic code of offspring speciation the formation of a new species through evolution

**species**
a group of the same organisms that can successfully reproduce with each other

**specificity**
usually refers to a DNA that codes for a specific trait

**sperm**
male gamete or sex cell that carries half the genetic material from the father

stability
maintaining a constant and healthy state of being

**steady state**
maintaining a constant and healthy state of being; similar to equilibrium

**stimulus**
changes in internal or external environment that cause an organisms response

**subunits**
molecules that make up DNA codes

**synthesis**
to combine several parts to create a whole

T

**template**
serves as a pattern for the construction of proteins and DNA

**testes**
male reproductive organs that produce sperm cells

**testosterone**
major male steroid hormone (a protein); involved with sex cells

**toxins**
a substance that causes harm to organisms

transport
a life function; refers to the distribution of nutrients through an organism

## U

**uterus**
reproductive organ where the developing embryo is implanted

## V

**vaccinations**
a small dose or weakened amount of a specific virus that is injected to prepare the immune system to fight a specific disease

**variation**
a change from the original; usually refers to sexual reproduction

**vector**
a virus that is used to "move" DNA fragments from one organism to another. (Used in biotechnology)

**viruses**
a pathogen whose only life function is to use a host to replicate

## W

**water cycle**
movement of water in and out of the environment throuh the process of precipitation, evaporation, and runoff.

**Watson-Crick model**
"a twisted ladder" model of the DNA proposed by James Watson and Francis Crick.

**White blood cell (leucocytes)**
blood cells that are involve in disease control

## X

**xylem**
a vascular tissue in plant in which water and other nutrients are transported from the root upward to other parts of the plant

## Y

**yolk**
nutrient rich substance found in mammalian eggs

**yolk sac**
the membrane surrounding the food supply of a yolk

## Z

**zygote**
a fertilized egg cell that is formed when two gametes join

**Cover colors:** Each of our book titles is printed in three different cover colors.

Same book title, same great contents, same price, three different cover colors to choose from.

Visit our site **SurvivingChem.com** to see all available cover colors for each title.

**Ordering Methods:**
**Online:** Survivingchem.com
**Fax/Phone:** (877) 224-0484
**Mail:** Send a completed Purchase Order Form with full or partial (half the order total ) payment to our address. Check payable to **E3 Scholastic Publishing.**

**Shipping: 10% shipping and handling charge** on all class orders.

# New York City Teachers:

## Our books are now on

## Famis e-catalog through Ingram

### Vendor #: ING032000

### Contract #: 7108108

E3 Scholastic Publishing is a Print-On-Demand publisher. Books are printed only when an order is placed.
All pre-paid class orders are processed, printed and shipped within a couple of days. We encourage schools and teachers to prepay for class-size orders to ensure that books are delivered by the time they are needed.

**Three convenient ways to Pre-Pay for your class-size orders:**
  1. Place your order from our website. Save Big and Pay Securely with a credit card through *PayPal.*
  2. Call us to request an online invoice. Just Click and Pay Securely with a credit card through *PayPal*
  3. Send a check for order total with your completed Purchase Order form. We also accept pre-payment of *half the order total.* We will invoice you the remaining amount after delivery.

Call or email us at any time with questions.

Made in the USA
Middletown, DE
18 January 2016